# The Spirit of Lao Tsu

## Masahisa Goi

### Translated by Robert Stevenson

# THE SPIRIT OF LAO TSU

## MASAHISA GOI

This book introduces eighteen of the original forty-eight chapters of *Rôshi Kôgi* (老子講義) by Masahisa Goi. Each offers a commentary on one chapter of Lao Tsu's *Dôtokukyô* (道徳経), also known as *Tao-te Ching*.

Original Japanese Edition:

老子講義　五井昌久著

白光真宏会出版本部 (白光出版)

1963年11月5日 (November 5, 1963)

English Edition:

The Spirit of Lao Tsu (英語版　老子講義)

五井昌久著　ロバート・スティブンソン訳

白光真宏会出版本部 (白光出版)

初版 2001年9月20日 (September 20, 2001)

English edition first published in Japan by

Byakko Press

812-1 Hitoana, Fujinomiya-shi

Shizuoka-ken, Japan, 418-0102

Translated from Japanese by Robert Stevenson.

Cover design by Michiko Watanabe

Production team: Paul H. Sherbow, Cathleen Turick, Kinuko Hamaya,
Volker Lenzner, Kai Neptune, David Lee Fish.

Printed in Japan by Eighty Eight Printing Co., Ltd.

ISBN 4-89214-143-7

Masahisa Goi
(1916-1980)

# About the Author

Born in Tokyo, Japan on November 22, 1916, Masahisa Goi was a poet, philosopher, writer and singer. Though he aimed at a career in music, he found himself spontaneously drawn to the realms of philosophy and spiritual guidance. In his autobiography, *One Who Connects Heaven and Earth* (publication pending), he explains that at the age of thirty he attained a state of oneness with his divine Self.

Mr. Goi authored more than fifty books and volumes of poetry, including *God and Man* (his first and most fundamental work), *How to Develop Your Spirituality, Catch the Light, The Way to the White Light, Lectures on the Bible,* and *Buddha and his Disciple. The Spirit of Lao Tsu* is the third of his books to be published in English, after *God and Man* and *The Future of Mankind.* Several others are now in the translation process.

Before departing from this world in 1980, Mr. Goi named Mrs. Masami Saionji, his adopted daughter, as his spiritual successor and leader of the world peace prayer movement that he initiated.

*Contents*

Prologue    13

1   The Nameless is the Beginning of Heaven and Earth   17
*(Dôtokukyô, Chapter 1)*

2   The Sage is in the Realm of No-action   26
*(Dôtokukyô, Chapter 2)*

3   It is not Known Whose Child I am
But I am the Image of what Came before the Ruler   37
*(Dôtokukyô, Chapter 4)*

4   Heaven and Earth are not Benevolent   46
*(Dôtokukyô, Chapter 5)*

5   Heaven is Eternal, Earth is Long   56
*(Dôtokukyô, Chapter 7)*

6   The Highest Good is Like Water   65
*(Dôtokukyô, Chapter 8)*

7   Practice the Void in the Extreme   77
*(Dôtokukyô, Chapter 16)*

8   That Which is Broken is Made Anew   87
*(Dôtokukyô, Chapter 22)*

9   Become the Same in Loss as the Person of Loss   97
*(Dôtokukyô, Chapter 23)*

10   Independent of it there is no Change,
     Wherever it is Practiced there is no Danger          106
     *(Dôtokukyô, Chapter 25)*

11   Nothing is Abandoned, Nothing is Discarded          116
     *(Dôtokukyô, Chapter 27)*

12   Return to the Unlimited                             126
     *(Dôtokukyô, Chapter 28)*

13   One who Knows Oneself is Enlightened                136
     *(Dôtokukyô, Chapter 33)*

14   The Way is Vast Yet can Move from Left to Right     147
     *(Dôtokukyô, Chapter 34)*

15   If you Take the Great Elephant Out into
     the World with You                                  158
     *(Dôtokukyô, Chapter 35)*

16   The Highest Virtue is not Virtuous
     Hold This and You have Virtue                       168
     *(Dôtokukyô, Chapter 38)*

17   The One of Old                                      178
     *(Dôtokukyô, Chapter 39)*

18   It is as if the Great Creation were Lacking         188
     *(Dôtokukyô, Chapter 45)*

Notes                                                   198

Organizations Honoring Masahisa Goi                     202

*Illustrations*

1. Masahisa Goi writing the name of
   Lao Tsu (*Rôshi* 老子) in Japanese                    11

2. No-action (*Mui* 無為)                                12
   Calligraphy by Masahisa Goi

3. Lao Tsu (*Rôshi* 老子)                                36
   Calligraphy by Masahisa Goi

4. *Kuu* (空)                                            76
   Calligraphy by Masahisa Goi

5. The Way is Vast (*Daidô* 大道)                        146
   Calligraphy by Masahisa Goi

Masahisa Goi writing the name of Lao Tsu (*Rôshi* 老子) in Japanese

No-action (*Mui* 無為)
Calligraphy by Masahisa Goi

*from within the midst of emptiness*
  *he appears*
*leading the eternal life itself*
  *the true person of freedom*

                    *Lao Tsu*

*describing the Way*
  *he supercedes it*
*enveloped in light*
  *he does not cling to it*

*empty-empty, still-still*
  *empty-still-still*
*He is*
  *total freedom in Mu-i*[1]

*unfathomable and vast*
  *his spirit*
*beyond time and space*
  *his strength*
*moving the very soul*
  *he links human beings to the universal origin*

*Lao Tsu now within me*

*his infinite echo draws near*

Lao Tsu is, as described in the poem above, a person of true freedom—a truly divine being. Indeed, the difference between this spirit of Lao Tsu, on the one hand, and the 'isms' or popular movements of today, on the other, is as great as that between the mud underfoot and the clouds overhead.

Achievement of true freedom requires total mastery of the way of *Mu-i* (No-action) taught by Lao Tsu. Only by such total mastery of this Way of *Mu-i* is it possible to lead the life which joins Heaven and Earth in a single, truly free spirit.

While I am by no means opposed to the intellectual activity of our modern era, I do remain unconvinced by the current lifestyle and academic knowledge of humanity, that continue to cause people to cling to peripheral forms while ignoring altogether the original essence of the universe and the source of the Life Force.

Lao Tsu's way of life is vital to the intellectual people of today. Convinced that they must live each day by thinking through each action with the cerebral brain alone, and clinging fiercely to the peripheral, modern human beings have forgotten what is, in fact, most important.

Lao Tsu wields words of illumination to teach human

beings about this most important 'something.' I, in turn, have attempted to interpret these words in my own fashion to make them more readily understood by the modern reader. I sincerely hope that these Lectures on Lao Tsu will assist the reader in bringing out his or her inner, divine Self, and in directly sensing the resonance of the universal source.

Masahisa Goi

Ichikawa, Japan

October 1963

# THE NAMELESS IS THE BEGINNING OF HEAVEN AND EARTH

*The way of ways is not the true Way.*

*The name of names is not the true Name.*

*The Nameless is the beginning of Heaven and Earth.*

*That with name is the mother of all creation.*

*Thus, with true Nothingness one may view the mystery,*

*And with true Being one may perceive the barrier.*

*These two are of the same origin, yet their names differ.*

*These two are called Profound.*

*Beyond the Profound lies the gateway to the Universal Mystery.*

*Dôtokukyô[2], Chapter 1*

*The way of ways is not the true Way.*

*The name of names is not the true Name.*

These lines are famous throughout the East, and I suppose there are many who, upon reading them, will recall having heard them previously. Few, however, probably know their author.

The totally free and unobstructed way of life that is, indeed, the very essence of Lao Tsu is expressed in these opening words. Their meaning might be summarized as follows: originally that which is called Life was entirely free and capable of any number of things. But if a particular way or name becomes attached to this, the Life Force becomes restricted, and it is impossible to conduct activities outside of that single form. Life's initially free nature is, thus, no longer given expression. Similarly, the Life Force can become fettered when placed within the confines of the fixed name of a person or organization.

At the center of a human being lies the same Life Force that is the focus of Lao Tsu's opening two lines, and we, too, were thus all originally made capable of accomplishing anything in perfect freedom. But if a person clings to a set way, that way will itself grasp hold of one's spirit and, regardless of how great a way it may appear to be, the original freedom of the Life Force will be restricted. The same holds true for names: once a name is affixed to something, the Life Force ceases to function outside the limits of that particular appellation.

Human beings were not initially placed within these kinds of confines, and originally had no need to cling to things in order to exist. Even if one clings with only the slightest strength, the true way will remain hidden, as will the brilliant original nature of the true name cease to shine forth. Lao Tsu was a person who disliked clinging more than anything else, and one finds lessons on the primordially free nature of life throughout his many and varied works.

In the course of all of our lives there are, however, many things, such as the laws of society and the doctrines of religions, that can slow the otherwise free-flowing movements of the world about us. Thus, through narrow-mindedness and rigidity, human beings forfeit their freedom and cause the once animated beauty of life to stagnate.

God's divine spirit can be revealed in the way of religion, but once a religion is identified as 'The Way,' the original freedom of the divine spirit is lost. In other words, the way people speak when they proclaim dogma such as 'This is the way' is not really worthy of mention. The true Way is free change itself, and becomes manifest in the natural and sincere actions of each and every person.

It is, for this reason, a mistake to force a religious way on others, or to describe religion with words alone. Indeed, to force religion upon others only smothers the profound flavor of the divine spirit in a distasteful, often unpalatable, crust of empty rhetoric. The true Way will only reveal itself when each individual leads a life of sincere practice, thereby joining in a natural manner with the spirit of divinity itself.

The same applies to names as well. We all hold a variety of names and titles as a consequence of having been born into a world composed of innumerable groups, organizations, corporations, and so forth. Numerous as the titles are, they represent little more than the superficial appellations affixed by the various people and organizations themselves. They have nothing to do with the true name that remains far below the surface, concealed.

A person's true name refers to what is more commonly called his or her heavenly mission or divine purpose in life. A person's mission may be expressed in this world through a name or title but, Lao Tsu cautions, this does not mean that we should attach ourselves to such names. Once attached to a single title, it becomes impossible to express the true name, and the mission that lies beneath can easily be left unfulfilled.

*The Nameless is the beginning of Heaven and Earth.*
*That with name is the mother of all creation.*

The Nameless—that without name—is the source of the

energy used to create the universe. The Nameless is the origin of the positive force that works behind everything that existed prior to the appearance of all relativistic phenomena.

This creative force and ultimate power that pervades the universe has been termed many things over the ages. It has been referred to as 'God' or the 'Omnipotent' by some, and the 'Great Life Force,' 'Creator,' or 'Way' by others. The fact that this Great Life Force has gone by such a variety of names underscores an important, if often forgotten, point: for human beings to grasp the astronomical concept of the original energy source that lies behind everything, it is imperative that at least a temporary title be affixed. Without the use of names, people simply cannot comprehend.

This is why Lao Tsu adopts the term 'The Nameless.' And yet, even though called The Nameless, The Nameless is itself a title. It is to avoid the confusion caused by this paradox that I personally prefer to use the more direct term, 'God,' instead.

'God is the beginning of Heaven and Earth.' Put in this more readily understandable form, the meaning of Lao Tsu's original lines are made clear. Heaven and Earth exist within God, and each represents a single manifestation of God's total being. It is important to realize, however, that the Heaven and Earth referred to here are not simply the blue sky and dark soil that we see when we gaze out upon the horizon. Lao Tsu speaks here about the deeper, spiritual

Heaven and Earth that express themselves via the sky and ground for us to appreciate. Encompassing the blue sky and earth outside, this spiritual Heaven and Earth extend within a human being as well, continually operating there as what is commonly referred to as 'Yin' and 'Yang.'[3]

People have a tendency to want to attach forms to the things about them, and it is for this reason that we often find people craving a visual image of God almost as soon as that name is attached. Fully aware of this predilection for forms, Lao Tsu avoids using the terms 'God' or 'Omnipotent' and opts, instead, for the neutral expression, 'The Nameless.'

And yet, once given a name, even The Nameless ceases to be nameless—ceases to be God itself—and exists as nothing more than a single manifestation of God instead. When a title is affixed, the fine spiritual wavelengths of The Nameless are gradually transformed into the coarser wavelengths of material phenomena. Put in Lao Tsu's words, that which possesses a name then gives birth to the 'Ten Thousand Things' and becomes the mother of all creation.

Take, for example, the distinction between a dishtowel and a rag used for dusting. The same piece of cloth can be applied to either chore, yet becomes locked into its role as one or the other as soon as it is decided that one is to be a dishtowel and the other a dust-rag. The respective roles of dishtowel and dust-rag are thus determined the instant a relativistic name is attached. Obviously not limited to dishtowels and dust-rags, other objects are similarly restricted by their titles as well.

Let us turn now to the final, and related, section.

*Thus, with true Nothingness one may view the mystery,*
*And with true Being one may perceive the barrier.*
*These two are of the same origin, yet their names differ.*
*These two are called Profound.*
*Beyond the Profound lies the gateway to the Universal Mystery.*

The expression 'true Nothingness' is used by Lao Tsu to point to the same thing that he does with the expression The Nameless: both refer to the divine reality, or 'God.' Within God is hidden the strange and wondrous. God is, for this reason, also called Omnipotent, Omniscient, and All-Able.

Just as it is possible for us to behold aspects of this divine Reality itself, we can also discern 'barriers' or distinctions in the ways in which this Reality manifests itself. Lao Tsu goes on to say that because both are manifestations of the same, ultimate Reality, they differ in name only.

Both, on the other hand, can be called Profound. The Profound is the phenomenal representation of the Omnipotent, Omniscient, and mysterious spiritual existence of God Itself. Timeless and possessing infinite depth and width, this mysterious spiritual entity called 'the Profound' by Lao Tsu is, likewise, said to have given birth to all creation.

Indeed, nothing is more difficult than trying to describe God. When writing a manuscript such as this, one is faced with the all-but-impossible task of wielding the written word to depict something invisible and untouchable, and capable of instantly taking on an infinitely grand or minuscule form. In short, one cannot escape from having to rely upon phenomenal forms when describing God to others. As a consequence, people are often left puzzled after listening to the incredible rhetoric philosophers and others frequently resort to when attempting to depict the Divine, and all that they retain from it is a vague sense of satisfaction over having added to the store of their knowledge.

A simple review of some of the terms used by Lao Tsu to describe The Divine (God) should be more than adequate to convince the reader of the enormity of this problem. Take, for example, the character *gen* (玄) in Japanese. By itself, *gen* means profound, mysterious, or sublime. It may also be combined with the character for 'person' (*hito* 人), to form the compound 'expert' (*kurôto* 玄人). The expert is the master of a given way and therefore holds the highest and most magnificent powers in that way. Remove the 'person' from this compound, and we are left with *gen* alone—the highest being in every and all ways. We are, in short, left with God.

Yet human beings cannot fully comprehend the reality

of God via the small, individual self. Only when one discards the restricted self and becomes Emptiness (*Kuu* 空) itself is it possible to enter deep within the divine spirit of God. Lao Tsu concludes by stating that this Emptiness can be either shallow or deep. Whether shallow or deep, it is, nevertheless, Profound.

# Chapter 2

# THE SAGE IS IN THE REALM OF NO-ACTION

*If everyone under Heaven knows what makes beauty beautiful,*

*This can only be bad.*

*If everyone knows what makes the good good,*

*This can only be evil.*

*Being and nothingness live side by side,*

*Troubles and ease are together made.*

*Short is used to measure long,*

*High and low each other face,*

*Noise and voice in mutual harmony sound,*

*Before and after together yield.*

*The Sage that takes hold of this lives in the realm of*

*No-action, and teaches the lesson of no words.*

*It made the Ten Thousand Things*

*But does not speak.*

*It gives birth*

*But does not own.*

*It performs*

*But does not rely upon.*
*It achieves*
*But is not present.*
*Only this has no presence.*
*Take hold of this, and you will not part.*

Dôtokukyô, *Chapter 2*

The meaning of this chapter may be summarized in a single phrase: the Sage[4] is one who has gone beyond the relativistic world and resides in the realm of No-action without attaching himself[5] to any things, circumstances or events. He is not proud of having performed this feat on his own, nor does he focus his attention there; regardless of the energies expended, he does not cling to his achievements. To exist in this realm of the Sage means to spare others trouble and to reside within their hearts forever. Lao Tsu is here describing this free and unrestricted realm of spiritual liberation within which the Sage dwells.

To have a sense of beauty, it is also necessary to have a sense for the form of its relative opposite, ugliness. To know good is also to know that bad stands in contrast to it. Everything prior to *The Sage that takes hold of this* in this chapter describes this relativistic world, and this is why we find 'being' placed with 'nothingness,' 'troubles' with 'ease,'

27

'short' with 'long,' 'high' with 'low,' and 'before' with 'after.'

*Mu-i* (無為 No-action) is the most important single word used in this chapter. Just what is the meaning of *Mu-i* (No-action) as used here?

*Mu-i* is used in everyday Japanese speech in the expression 'to remain idle and do nothing but eat.' This is, however, very different from Lao Tsu's *Mu-i*.

There are those Lao Tsu specialists who depict him as a pessimist and view his philosophy as negativistic because of this concept of *Mu-i*. Such interpretations do not do Lao Tsu service. Lao Tsu was a divine being who far surpassed the relative terms of optimism or pessimism and who acted in this world from the deepest-of-deep, emptiest-of-empty realms at the root of the Great Life Force itself.

When describing this to others, Lao Tsu spoke in a completely natural manner without imposing ideas of 'should' or 'must.' In this way, Lao Tsu's every word and action was converted into light which was, in turn, cast upon others and on the rest of the world about him.

The Great Life Force moves on its own in an animated fashion—this is the essence of Lao Tsu. Knowing this, I feel I understand Lao Tsu and, while it is impossible to express with words or pen, I sense the intense waves of life-energy that flow from Lao Tsu now sinking deep into my own body.

'Do this,' 'do that,' 'you must do it this way'—this is

how things operate with most people in the world today. The true Sage, on the other hand, always acts as a medium for the laws of divine and spiritual worlds, transmitting them via his or her material body to the physical world. Never does the Sage act upon the orders of the physical brain. This is how one acts in No-action, how one resides in *Mu-i.*

Even in the case of the physical body, the heart, lungs, stomach, and other organs do not operate upon the conscious command of our brains, but function naturally on their own, for as long as we remain healthy. Our thoughts should operate in the same natural manner. Somewhere along the line, though, thoughts have become separated from the various physical organs of the body.

The problem of thoughts becoming separate from the body may be readily understood from the following example: if one were to focus one's thoughts only upon one's heart, it is most probable that one would suffer some disorder. The same holds true for all of the other organs—lungs, intestines, liver, and so on. The most healthy times are those in which no thoughts are being focused on the various organs whatsoever.

Even if people do not generally think it true, it is precisely the same with the spirit. People generally fall into a deep melancholy whenever they attempt to consciously move their spirit to achieve a goal they feel they must accomplish.

As a result, they handle everything with the accumulated experience stored in their memories; what is more, most think this to be the natural human condition.

The fact is, however, that virtually all the sages and saints of old—not just Lao Tsu—rejected the practice of relying upon cerebral knowledge and turning things over and over in one's head prior to taking action. Why? Because, just as Lao Tsu says, it is impossible for humanity to fully separate itself from the pain of this relativistic world using the limited knowledge of the physical brain alone.

For the average person, though, this might sound preposterous. Most people feel that we are unable to act until we have engendered the action within our physical brain. But Lao Tsu is not speaking as an ordinary, unawakened person. Lao Tsu is speaking here as a Sage, and it is here that the fundamental difference between Sage and unawakened person is made strikingly clear. What appears impossible to the unawakened person is a matter of no concern to the Saint or Sage. Regardless of how good a job an unawakened person may do in deceiving others into believing that they reside in this realm of *Mu-i*, the flaws in their half-baked enlightenment will surface in time, and their students will begin to question if their teacher's are truly the actions of No-action. Thus, in the end, one will fall far below the average people whom one has placed oneself so high above.

To live in the realm of No-action is by no means easy to

realize in practice, and here arises the quite natural doubt of how such a life is possible.

Most think that it is because of our ability to plan, conduct jobs, and manage affairs with others using the intellect that the individual is then able to lead a normal life. There are even those angered by talk of No-action, who say that all position and wealth are products of constant planning; a life without thinking things over or planning is, for these people, unthinkable. I suppose there are even those who wish to be spared such teachings, stating outright their opinion that there is no need for saints or sages, and that there is no possibility that they themselves could ever become one.

While certainly true of times past, the present is a particularly difficult age to be leading a Lao Tsu-ian life of No-action. One would think that, among the many Lao Tsu scholars who take pleasure in reading his words and appreciating these with their intellect, there would be some who realize that the true Lao Tsu exists prior to the words he left behind, and that it is the motions of his life force—the stream of light flowing from him—that is of primary importance. Few, however, show any real signs of understanding this truth. I am fortunate in being able to clearly see Lao Tsu as a river of life and an emitter of light; and yet, I am still frequently halted while writing these essays on Lao Tsu by the frustrating question of how to bring others to understand what Lao Tsu is really like. I think this true Lao Tsu is expressed most successfully by the poem 'Lao Tsu' which appears as the Prologue to this volume and in my anthology of poems entitled *Prayer*, but by no means do I believe that using prose to describe Lao Tsu is an easy task. One is plagued by the fact that the more one writes about Lao Tsu, the more one is confused by him. On the other hand, one is obliged to explain each of his words fully. When I try to tackle the single term *Mu-i* (No-action), for example, I find it all but impossible to express with pen alone the limitless depth and breadth of *Mu-i*, or the myriad worlds that continue endlessly to spring from it.

Setting this problem aside for the moment, however, let us move on to describe what practical steps the average person can take to enter this realm of No-action.

The first step towards this state of *Mu-i* is made when a person comes to believe in the existence and great love of God. Starting from this spirit of belief, the person walks, in complete entrustment, one step at a time down the path towards *Mu-i*.

I suggest that those not familiar with the term *Mu-i* (No-action) think of the famous passage 'Emptiness is all Things' that appears in the famous Hannya Sutra:

> *'Things' are all empty.*
> *Emptiness is all Things.*

As pointed out in my book *Love, Peace, and Prayer*, it would not be wrong to think of the second phrase, 'Emptiness is all Things,' as representing the same realm that is described by the term *Mu-i*.

What is responsible for disturbing people's fortunes is none other than the thoughts that fill the minds of all of us. It is thought waves, stirred by feelings of jealousy, hate, anger, sadness, and misfortune, that set the winds into motion; there is no misfortune or sadness intrinsic to human beings themselves. Does a person sense misfortune or sadness when sound asleep? Of course not. A person's thoughts leave the physical body when asleep and, while the body itself may continue to exist as before, no emotions arise while one is resting soundly.

The meaning of the above is that, if a person's thoughts are not placed within sadness and misfortune, the person will not experience sadness and misfortune at all. Buddhism thus focuses on exercises to eliminate these thoughts entirely and to enter the state called *Kuu*[6] (Emptiness).

Human beings, as I frequently point out, are not simply physical entities. On the contrary, the physical body is nothing more than a single manifestation of the resonance of the human spirit. Anyone who has conducted psycho-spiritual research will readily understand that a human being holds many other embodiments in addition to his physical one, and I think that those who understand and concentrate on the following can bring out their divinity rapidly:

1) More important than the peripheral (the physical) is that human beings live within the Great Life Force (God) as embodiments of bright light itself.

2) Human beings are existences who can freely manifest the world they wish for in their present surroundings as long as they refrain from latching onto their thoughts.

In Buddhism, people practice Zazen[7] to reach *Kuu* (Emptiness). It is true that this world can become divine by having everyone enter the state of *Kuu*, where we all thrive as manifestations of the bright spirit that flows therefrom. This is not, however, easy to achieve in practice.

This is where the action of prayer becomes necessary. By holding to the spirit of prayer and leading our daily lives with all of our thoughts thrown into the great love of the Divine Spirit of God, we may enter a spiritual state, unsoiled, and without pain, close to the realm of *Kuu*. Once having achieved that state, we will naturally come to dwell within the world of *Kuu* itself, and the wondrous life of acting in No-action will be cast open.

That is why, rather than fixing your thoughts on the state of *Mu-i*, towering high above from the very beginning, I think it is more natural to focus on a readily-achievable goal, such as the Prayer for World Peace. This is a way to awaken oneself and the rest of humanity at the same time. Transported by saving rays from the Divine World, everyone will, in time, naturally be moved into the realm of acting in No-action.

By living every day within the prayer for world peace, I believe that all people can be elevated into Lao Tsu's realm of *Mu-i*.

Lao Tsu (*Rôshi* 老子)
Calligraphy by Masahisa Goi

*Chapter 3*

# It is not Known Whose Child I am But I am the Image of what Came before the Ruler.

*The Way is like an empty vessel*

*Yet with use, it may not be filled.*

*Like the deep,*

*It is the forefather of the Ten Thousand Things.*

*It blunts the sharp and untangles disputes.*

*It tempers light, yet is the same as dust.*

*It exists like that which overflows.*

*It is not known whose child I am,*

*But I am the image of what came before the Ruler.*

*Dôtokukyô, Chapter 4*

In classical Chinese, the verses in this chapter are written like this. Difficult as it may seem, I think that Chinese writing has a special quality about it that is lost if presented in another fashion. Chinese writing seems to be particularly well-suited for lectures on religion or the Way. If one endeavors to read the words of Lao Tsu or of others in their original form, their true spirit becomes perfectly clear without any need for rearrangement or translation whatsoever.

Present-day human beings have become extremely numb to the effect of written images, however, because of their desire for a cerebral understanding of everything they come into contact with. Rather than decide issues instinctively with our hearts, we tend to judge things rationally with the knowledge stored in our brain. One might even conclude that this favoring of the cerebral over the instinctual is, in fact, a distinguishing characteristic of society in general today.

Moving on to our discussion of the chapter itself, this fourth chapter in Lao Tsu's book *Dôtokukyô* describes the person who has made the Way a part of oneself, and it likewise depicts the true being of Lao Tsu.

Let us turn now to a step-by-step analysis of each portion of this chapter.

*The Way is like an empty vessel,*
*Yet with use, it may not be filled.*

Many interpret the words 'empty vessel' as 'it will not fill' or simply 'empty;' Lao Tsu, however, uses this term to express something far more profound than merely 'not full.' Just as *Kuu* (空), commonly considered to mean 'emptiness', does not simply mean 'empty' or 'nothing' in Buddhism, so, too, does *chû* (沖) (empty plate, pitcher or vessel) here represent what in the world of words is undefinable, what in the world of shapes is immeasurable, and what, when reached for or grabbed at, proves intangible.

Lao Tsu goes on to say that when one then tries to make use of this Way—when one attempts, in other words, to make manifest the workings of the Life Force of God—its uses will be unlimited. There will never be too much for it and it may, thus, never be filled completely.

*Like the deep,*
*It is the forefather of the Ten Thousand Things.*

These two lines evoke the immeasurable depth and tranquility of the Way, the source of all things in existence. They let us sense the great power that resides at the inner depths of the deep and silent.

Between the lines, these words tell of the way of life which must inevitably be taken by those who have attained the Way. I will attempt to clarify this step by step while making reference to the well-know phrase *Wakôdôjin*[8] (和光

39

同塵—'soften the light so that it may mingle with the dust').

*It blunts the sharp and untangles disputes.*
*It tempers light, yet is the same as dust.*

To 'blunt the sharp' and to 'temper light' here mean for the person who has mastered the Way to soften his or her knowledge and talents and thus not expose the keen edge of the Self. One must, in this way, settle disputes and handle all matters as smoothly as a needle being passed through a piece of cloth.

Or, using the light metaphor, Lao Tsu cautions us against harshly focusing light upon people when shining forth the light of God, and warns that it is important to adjust this light to appropriately match each and every individual. One should always radiate a soft and peaceful light that shines as evenly upon the unfortunate—those immersed in 'dust'—as it does upon the gifted or fortunate. This passage thus teaches that the light of harmony shines equally upon the pure and impure—the famous lesson of *Wakôdôjin*.

It is important that we, too, avoid the tendency of, on the one hand, preaching or talking down to others on the pretense that we understand while, on the other hand, conversing freely only with those who hold the same beliefs as our own. We must always think of the other's position, and

join with them in heart, striving in the spirit of consideration to communicate with new people of a wide variety of
social strata.

Indeed, there are many cases of people pursuing the
Way even though they do not begin with that as their objec-
tive, and there are even examples of people beginning on
the Way while they appear on the surface to be seeking
nothing more than simple utilitarian ends. It must be
remembered that, regardless of what ends the individual
may be seeking, deep within him or her there is a person in
pursuit of the Way. It is thus our duty to listen to even the
most superficial talk of utilitarian phenomena, in addition
to what one might consider to be more interesting or meaningful discussions.

It may also be said that the same Way that leads one
person to enlightenment ceases to be the true Way once it is
forced upon others as the *only* way. Why? Because such a
way only becomes a restrictive nuisance when viewed from
the position of the other, causing him or her to gradually
turn against it.

The Way is the working of the Life Force of God Itself
and, with everything inside its limitless spirit, it is a path
that anyone may easily enter upon. It is not, therefore, the
kind of thing that need be forced on people. Simply inform-
ing people that they are already treading upon it should be
adequate explanation in and of itself. As divisions, or por-

tions, of the Life Force of God, all are God's children. As children of God, we are all equal. There are no differences in Life itself.

When it comes to life in the human world, however, distinctions arise between upper and lower, superior and inferior, and so forth. If one then asks what it was that imposed these distinctions of high and low, superior and inferior, upon human life in the first place, one is forced to conclude that this must have been something other than the Life Force Itself.

Put simply, all of these distinctions result from the lingering echoes of human thoughts. Thoughts that impede one's own life likewise interfere with the lives of others. This is why I am always urging people to return all thoughts, via prayer, to the divine spirit of God, to revert to our original form as part of the Divine Life Force, and to complete our worldly missions. Lao Tsu is one who mastered this truth.

We are brought now to the next and final line—a line that contains all of the magnitude and incredible vivacity of which Lao Tsu is capable.

*It is not known whose child I am,*
*but I am the image of what came before the Ruler.*

Lao Tsu refers to the Way as 'I' in this passage. If one is not careful, it is easy to make the mistake of interpreting this 'I' to mean only 'Way.' If this were the case, Lao Tsu would have said something like 'whose child is the Way' or 'it is not known whose child the Way is,' for example. Lao Tsu does not use 'Way' here, but intentionally uses the word 'I' instead. We may gain a glimpse of the truly phenomenal scale of Lao Tsu if we go on to consider his use of the word 'I' here in a bit more detail.

Lao Tsu, as I have written elsewhere, is a person who expresses the eternal Life Force. It may actually be best to consider him as someone who appeared in this world in order to represent this eternal Life Force. For this reason, Lao Tsu describes himself as none other than the Way by using 'Way' interchangeably with 'I' in this chapter. Put in another way, Lao Tsu here is saying that he is one with God. His was a supreme faith—no, the term 'supreme faith' is not necessary in Lao Tsu's case, for Lao Tsu's was a far more basic and fundamental spirit that made faith a matter of course, something totally natural. According to Lao Tsu, the Way is the Self itself. Lao Tsu exists as a person at one with the great Life Force of God. The Way is, thus, not something separate from Lao Tsu and, just as Lao Tsu is the Way, the Way is Lao Tsu.

It is this natural spirit that calls the Way 'I', that says 'It is not known whose child I am,' and that states that this is a manifestation of the absolute being, God. Given this, the phrase that follows, 'but I am the image of what came before the Ruler,' becomes a truism as well.

The word 'ruler' as used in China meant 'person at the center of the empire.' We are here given yet another glimpse of Lao Tsu's true magnanimity as he challenges the common conception of ruler by stating that there exists something prior to the 'person at the center of the empire.' Lao Tsu states clearly that this something is the Way, in other words, Lao Tsu himself.

The Way is, for Lao Tsu, the origin of everything. To say that the Way stands prior to all images and objects means that all the universe moves atop of it, i.e., atop the divine spirit and works of the Absolute Being (Universal God). While the universe moves ultimately according to the infinite wisdom of the Universal God, the Universal God does not directly involve itself in this, but, rather, manages everything via the various divinities and spirits. All of the divinities that appear in Japan's Kojiki[9], for instance, were in this way named for their particular function. Some even have distinct personalities as well.

In this sense, it is interesting to note that no historical traces remain for those who wish to explain Lao Tsu as someone who was born into this world as a normal child, underwent various acetic practices and, as a result, entered the path of enlightenment. Unlike the Buddha, Christ, Confucius, and many other famous saints and sages who left various oral and written records behind, Lao Tsu was virtually ignored by all historical chronicles.

Why? Because, as Lao Tsu is saying to me as I sit here in my room at this moment, he was not a physical human being born, as others are, of physical parents, but was a person of spiritual body, a divine being able to appear at any time, any place. This is also why Lao Tsu can identify himself with the Way, just as it is perfectly natural for the historical figure Buddha—born as a physical person into this world—to say 'I am the Buddha of the greatest victory, the Buddha of the greatest wisdom.'

*Chapter 4*

# HEAVEN AND EARTH
# ARE NOT BENEVOLENT

*Heaven and Earth are not benevolent;*

*They treat the Ten Thousand Things as straw dolls.*

*The sage is not benevolent;*

*He treats the commoners[10] as straw dolls.*

*The space between Heaven and Earth is*

*like that inside of the bellows:*

*Empty, it may not be exhausted;*

*The more it moves the more it ushers forth.*

*Many words, though, cause it to jam.*

*Best, then, to protect the middle.*

*Dôtokukyô, Chapter 5*

*Heaven and Earth are not benevolent;*
*They treat the Ten Thousand Things as straw dolls.*
*The sage is not benevolent;*
*He treats the commoners as straw dolls.*

Heaven and Earth did not spawn the myriad of things by first drafting a plan or devising a theory. Heaven and Earth are, instead, continuously giving birth to and extinguishing things, in a perfectly natural way. This is not to say that they act out of malevolence, but simply means that they treat the Ten Thousand Things (i.e., all of creation) as 'straw dolls.'[11] The Sage—whose outstretched hand does not attempt to save the commoner (i.e., unawakened person), but naturally leaves him in his discarded condition—likewise seems to act out of a similar attitude of disinterest.

The above describes the superficial meaning of the opening lines of this chapter. The teaching of Lao Tsu contained within these words, however, is that Heaven and Earth do not create and destroy things in accordance with the individual wishes of human beings. Rather, the power of Heaven and Earth simply follows the laws of nature, executing these laws as they are.

If, on the other hand, the movements of the universe were carried out by a Heaven and Earth that had some sort of plan or that possessed consciousness of self, these laws would be thrown into disorder every time something occurred apart from the main line of the all-encompassing activities of the Universal God. Disruption of the laws of the universe would mean that the unity of things would be destroyed, that this world would be cast into disarray, and that the very existence of the Ten Thousand Things themselves would be imperiled. This is why Lao Tsu says it is best that Heaven and Earth do not practice selfish affection separate from the spirit of the Universal God.

Just think of what it would be like if Heaven and Earth had an ego and controlled everything according to their own likes and preferences. The rain falls and the wind blows in accordance with the laws of nature, but this does not mean that they represent the willful spirit of Heaven and Earth.

The laws of nature apply equally to humankind. Thought waves emitted from one's own self, for example, join with other waves and return in similar form some time later in one's life, as suggested by such sayings as 'Hate and Be Hated,' 'Hit and Be Hit,' and similar adages.

Thus, a person's fate is totally of his or her own making, and it is quite absurd to think that one's misfortunes were created by someone else.

On the other hand, it sometimes happens that even though one may try hard to do good things for someone else, one's actions are not appreciated by the other person no matter how assiduously one may work on their behalf. This is either because the motive behind one's actions is still impure and lacks genuine concern for the other, or because one has a heavy karmic debt to that person from a previous lifetime. If the latter is the case, it is important to devote oneself more and more to working for the other person's happiness, or else to pray for the person's missions to be accomplished.

Just as individuals create their own futures with their own thoughts, so, too, does humanity construct its own circumstances. Even large-scale occurrences like natural disasters are brought about by the thoughts and actions of human beings.

The universal laws and the laws governing thought waves are thus immovable. Therefore, if one wants to alter one's fate, one must put one's thoughts and actions on the track of the Universal Law. In other words, one needs to attune one's thoughts and actions to the vibrations of the Universal God.

Next, we should address the question of what kind of lifestyle the Sage leads. Simply stated, the Sage exists just as Heaven and Earth do, never imposing thoughts of self upon others while functioning in a totally natural manner. This is why the Sage remains undisturbed, even by the sight of farmers laboring at their jobs. He is only moved by the spirit of nature. To the average person, however, he appears to be lacking compassion.

The Sage can discern the way of life that is best suited to each individual; his mission is to awaken people to the true spirit of God while they are in the process of extinguishing their karma from past lifetimes.

If one attempts to uplift people who have wandered from the Universal Law only by relieving their current suffering—while doing nothing to reorient them towards their true path—the results will not be true or lasting. The value of the Sage thus lies in his teaching people how to bring out the essential divine Self, while living and working within the particular situation in which each of them has been placed, so that they naturally extract themselves from their karmic ways of life.

The Sage is empty of all thoughts of self and, living within the lifestyle of *Mu-i* he or she interacts with others in a perfectly natural manner. To live in a perfectly natural way means that the light of the Universal God shines forth to the rest of us as well; the simple fact of the Sage's presence is a definite plus for others.

A great benevolence shines from deep within what at first glance appears to be an uncaring way of life.

*The space between Heaven and Earth is*
*like that inside of the bellows:*
*Empty, it may not be exhausted;*

*The more it moves the more it ushers forth.*

The 'bellows' referred to here is the same as that used by the blacksmith. The space between Heaven and Earth is just like the empty box that lies within the bellows: the harder the bellows is pumped, the stronger the breeze that comes from inside. An inexhaustible breeze comes from within something totally empty.

The Way between Heaven and Earth is similar to this. It, too, appears to be a vacuum, empty. Its strength is, however, inexhaustible and immeasurable. In a word, the power of Heaven and Earth is truly infinite.

*Many words, though, cause it to jam.*
*Best, then, to protect the middle.*

Heaven and Earth possess an infinite power that, when exerted, has no end. This power is not the sort of strength that can be recklessly discharged at will, however, and it is always employed according to the laws of the universe.

Upon gaining even the slightest power, human beings, on the other hand, immediately want to see it applied. With knowledge of only a fraction of the whole, a human being wants to run out and announce the newly gained 'wisdom' to all. The chatterbox does not hold any influence over people, though, and the more the person talks the deeper becomes his or her plight.

While possessing the same immeasurable power as Heaven and Earth, it is important that we exert this power in a way that matches each particular time and place. We must, in short, live by 'protecting the middle.'

It is not easy to defend the middle in practice, however, and there are few actually capable of doing so. Lao Tsu addresses his teachings to other awakened people and, as a result, those teachings seem impossible to achieve when directly conveyed to the average person. This is why I continue to give lessons in Lao Tsu, and labor to lay a gentle path to the Way of the Sages.

The Mean or Middle is a term that frequently appears in Confucius as well. Human beings have a difficult time protecting the middle, and constantly veer left or right.

The primary meaning of this chapter is that, just as Heaven and Earth move in accordance with the laws of nature so, too, does the Sage submerge his ego and live perfectly naturally within the spirit of the Universal God.

Special emphasis is thus placed on the fact that a perfectly natural way of life does not favor left or right, is beyond the grasp of all karmic thoughts, and protects the middle.

Observing the Japanese political arena, for example, we find that almost everyone seems to be either a conservative, a communist, or a socialist. Indeed, it appears that not a single politician who 'protects the middle' stands atop the podium today.

Perhaps this is why I am frequently left feeling that the people of this world put faith only in self-important types who capriciously tell others to go this way or that while at the same time turning a deaf ear to the voice of a person of truth, calling from a realm far beyond the waves of karmic thoughts to awaken them. Just as Lao Tsu teaches that the Sage's handling of the ordinary person as a 'straw doll' is only at first glance malevolent, so does the person who speaks of the way to develop one's original, divine spirit refrain from pointing a finger at others and telling them to act in any particular manner. Nor does he or she manage things for their benefit. We ought to live by avoiding, as much as possible, handling others as straw dolls, opting instead to promote a method that helps people bring out their intrinsic divinity while opening the way for the mission of humanity. This method is prayer for world peace.

A person with this singular focus on prayer will not veer to the left or right but is, instead, someone who protects the middle. This is because prayer is the act of casting all thoughts into the spirit of God—that is to say, of immersing all thoughts deep within one's inner, divine spirit. The self that has, in this way, been thrown inside the spirit of God is no longer tossed about by waves of karmic thoughts.

Perfectly naturally, it becomes, instead, a self enlivened

by new life from the spirit of God. One who lives within the spirit of prayer at all times—even if unable to attain the perfection of a sage such as Lao Tsu, who is beyond the act of prayer altogether—can, at any moment, perform actions close to those of the Sage with surprising ease.

It is difficult, however, to practice 'protection of the middle' in today's complex political and social conditions. Rather than starting with phrases like 'defend the middle,' it is important to take the first steps down the path that is naturally created whenever a person adopts an attitude of 'protecting the middle.' This way is the way of the Prayer for World Peace.

'World Peace,' of course, means Great Harmony. The way to World Peace resonates in perfect unison with the spirit of the Universal God, favoring neither left nor right, and protecting the middle. It is a path that all of humanity aspires to.

The movement for world peace through prayer is the true Way of the Middle. Rather than concentrate on difficult theoretical terms used to describe the teachings of the Sages of old, all of the lessons of the Sages will come alive for you if you simply entrust your life to the singular thought of prayer.

Direct translations of Lao Tsu's text tend to be of little benefit to most. Even if people read him or listen to lectures such as these, most are left feeling 'Oh, so that is what Lao

Tsu's about. But that's of no use to me.' Direct translations seem to offer little direction to the lives of most people.

That is why I have taken Lao Tsu's elevated and profound teachings, brought them down to a more readily understandable level, and, naturally blending with them, have laid their meaning bare for all.

Humanity lives at the crossroads of the ideals of Heaven (the vertical plane) and the realities of Earth (the horizontal plane). The Way of life is to Protect the Middle; the method is to pray the prayer for world peace.

*Chapter 5*

# HEAVEN IS ETERNAL, EARTH IS LONG

*Heaven is eternal, Earth is long.*
*The reason for their longevity—*
　*they do not think to create themselves.*
*The Sage who holds to this puts himself behind and is, thus, first.*
*Puts his body outside and, thus, exists within.*
*Is it not he without self who is well made?*

*Dôtokukyô, Chapter 7*

*Heaven is eternal, Earth is long.*

*The reason for their longevity—*

   *they do not think to create themselves.*

Heaven and Earth are said to be timeless because they have no self, No-action (*Mu-i* 無為) and no-intentions (*Mu-shin* 無心). Heaven does not hold any thoughts of itself as Heaven, nor does Earth wish to exist as Earth. Heaven and Earth are totally devoid of any ego that wishes to show itself or emphasize its own existence, and only serve in their roles as Heaven and Earth because that is what the spirit of the Universal God indicated they should do.

Not having a self apart from the heart of the Universal God, Heaven and Earth exist as the very spirit of the Universal God. This is why there is no ephemeral beginning or end when speaking of Heaven or Earth; this is why they are called timeless.

If the people of this world raise their eyes up to the vast reaches of the heavens in times of worry, brooding, or concern, the finite being called the self will be immediately absorbed within the unlimited depths of the spirit of Heaven and its timeless work, becoming a vast and deep spirit just like that of Heaven, leaving worldly cares behind. This is the spirit about which the Emperor Meiji[12] wrote in the following poem:

*The spring sky overhead—*
*May my spirit be as vast as its reaches.*

Turning next to consider the blessings bestowed by the great Mother Earth, one is struck by its unbounded, completely selfless love. Without receiving any reward from us, Mother Earth continually gives birth and sustains the many things essential to our existence. Untarnished, un-proud, and unselfish, the deep spirit of Heaven and Earth continually embraces mankind within its merciful heart.

Viewed against the great love of the Universal God responsible for having created this Heaven and Earth, one cannot help but laugh over human beings' trivial feuds and constant arguments over the most minor of issues.

The present divided condition of the nations of this world—countries working only to extend their own borders while threatening one another with all manner of military technology—is contrary to the spirit of God. This is, moreover, in direct opposition to the spirit of No-action/no-desire of Heaven and Earth.

*The Sage who holds to this puts himself behind and is, thus, first.*
*Puts his body outside and thus exists within.*
*Is it not he without self who is well made?*

Ultimately, all human beings are meant to live the lifestyle of the Sage. Yet I imagine most may have difficulty in understanding Lao Tsu's original words. Permit me, then, to explain this passage in some greater detail.

A person who is capable of leading the life of Heaven and Earth described in the previous passage is called a Sage. Put another way, the Sage is Heaven and Earth expressed via the human form.

Lao Tsu states that the Sage 'puts his body outside.' This phrase is usually interpreted as describing the life of placing others first, while putting one's own benefit second. Much is lost in this kind of standardized interpretation, however.

The truly profound teaching contained in the words 'puts his body outside' is that by giving second place to the interests of the physical self, a human being is then able to lead a life in which the true body—the Spiritual Body, the body that exists as a part of the Universal Life Force—is placed first.

Just as Heaven and Earth are expressions of the everlasting life force, so, too, is a human being a manifestation of this everlasting and eternal life energy. A person's true form is eternal life itself. The Spiritual Body is this eternal life. Divided among everyone, this eternal life force works throughout the universe to help manifest the spirit of the Universal God.

One of the functions of this Spiritual Body is to manifest itself in the material world as the physical body. It is when we forget that the physical body is only a manifestation of the Spiritual Body and begin thinking that humans are no more than their physical bodies that all trouble and strife present in the world today first emerge.

The person called the Sage knows well the origin of this trouble and lives with the physical self subordinate, the Spiritual Body primary. The life of the physical body will, in turn, be freely lived once the Spiritual Body takes first place.

As the reader has probably already discerned, the words that follow:

*...and, thus, exists within.*
*Is it not he without self who is well made?"*

mean that it is important to place the physical body outside of the soul and to work according to the spirit transmitted via the Spiritual Body. The Spiritual Body works as the spirit of God, and is actually just like Heaven and Earth: selfless. Acting out of this Spiritual Body (or, putting the same expression into my own terms—acting out of the divine Self) the individual can lead a splendid, yet settled, life. Using Buddhist terminology, this is called a perfectly free body and soul.

To return to the essential, divine Self and overcome the tendency of favoring the physical, it is necessary to restore the physical body to its original position—to 'put the body on the outside.' It is necessary to practice living as the Spiritual Body itself without dwelling on the physical.

If one had come to this world directly in the Spiritual Body (as did Lao Tsu), putting these teachings into practice would pose no problem. But, for most, living with the physical self 'on the outside' presents an extremely difficult task. Regardless of how difficult, however, it is essential that we lead the kind of life Lao Tsu describes if we are to develop as well-rounded individuals and complete ourselves as people of truth.

The universe is infinitely wide and infinitely deep. The number of planets similar to earth is, likewise, unlimited. Lately, an increasing amount of attention has been focused (even on this planet) upon the universe. Leaving aside the question of motives, the U.S.-Soviet space race has, in this sense, been a good thing. As a consequence, we now live in an age in which it is absolute nonsense to pretend that there is no relation between life on earth and life on other planets.

The earth is not alone, and all the stars and planets in the universe exist together mutually affecting one another. This is the same in principle as the way in which the nations of this planet coexist, mutually influencing one another, regardless of whether or not each is aware that this is in fact the case.

Our field of vision is gradually expanding and, in contrast with the parochial people of old who lived out their lives without ever venturing beyond the borders of their immediate neighborhoods, the attention of people today has spread, not only beyond their homes, but to other nations as well. This broadening awareness is just now beginning to include all of the universe. While it is true that, as one person pointed out to me the other day, some people still find the idea of consulting the rest of the universe of little benefit in settling our own earthly disorders, such people can only be termed ignorant of the true interconnectedness of the universe. Just as decisions in the U.S. can have an immediate, and powerful, impact on Japan, so, too, can the movements of the universe have an impact on the future of this planet as well.

Lao Tsu, Shakyamuni[13], and Jesus knew well this principle of interconnectedness, and their teachings were, in fact, all based on it. There are those who will denounce belief in such things as extraterrestrial beings, but it is certain that such life forms really do exist and are, moreover, constantly interacting with us. This truth was clearly taught by Shakyamuni and may be found in the many religious texts recorded by his followers.

I think it is time people freed themselves from such foolish ideas as that humans live only in this physical world, or that life exists only on this planet. Otherwise they will be limited to interpreting Lao Tsu and others' teachings as nothing more than idealistic descriptions of utopian conditions. Such people will thus be forced into casually denying the wisdom of Lao Tsu by saying that we cannot possibly realize such teachings in practice.

The teachings of Lao Tsu, Shakyamuni, and Jesus can be practiced. Until now, however, the motions of the universe have been composed of waves that have made it extremely difficult for humans to practice the truth. This is why I think that those who previously performed saintly deeds must have been truly outstanding figures.

Today, on the other hand, the natural movement of the universe is pushing the Earth into a higher position, one step closer to the heart of the Universal God; and accordingly, the disharmonious manifestations that I call karmic thought waves, which have been erupting all over the planet with tremendous vigor, are being rapidly extinguished. As a result, individuals or groups that attune their vibrations to the harmonious spirit of the Universal God will naturally be raised to a state where they can then operate more freely. Universal beings—angels of the universe—are now working to help speed this process.

It should be recalled that everything in this world exists in the form of waves and that there is, at this very moment, a movement underway to correct all waves that deviated from the Universal Laws—waves that have left the path of Universal Principles.

Lao Tsu's teachings point toward this path, and in all of

his works we can hear Lao Tsu saying 'Listen, everyone—it may require some effort to place yourselves upon the path of the universal law, but once you have overcome these hardships, do not swerve from the path. What kind of path is it? It's this kind.'

If, on the other hand, one places the physical body first, one will never ascend the path of the Universal Law. Rather than place the physical first, Lao Tsu, speaking from within me, is now saying to place that body behind, place it 'on the outside,' while putting development of one's spiritual being first. Only then will it be possible to help oneself, as well as to uplift the rest of this earthly world.

The most natural and easy means of putting the above into practice is via the Prayer for World Peace. Remember that the many forms of evil, misfortune, and misunderstanding of this physical world are in a constant process of vanishing, and that the path of the Universal Law passes directly through the Prayer for World Peace.

*Chapter 6*

# THE HIGHEST GOOD IS LIKE WATER

*The highest good is like water.*

*Water benefits the Ten Thousand Things, yet does not struggle.*

*It is in that which is despised by most—*

   *therefore it is close to The Way.*

*Land, when right, is a Residence*

*Deep, when right, is a Heart*

*Virtue, when right, is Giving*

*Belief, when right, is the Word*

*Order, when right, is Rule*

*Talent, when right, is Affairs*

*Time, when right, is Movement*

*Only this does not struggle—*

*It is, thus, never at blame.*

*Dôtokukyô, Chapter 8*

*The highest good is like water.*
*Water benefits the Ten Thousand Things, yet does not struggle.*
*It is in that which is despised by most—*
*therefore it is close to The Way.*

'The highest good,' as used in the original text, means the greatest of goods. The highest form of this, Lao Tsu says, is water. Water is the highest form of good because it benefits everything, but does not in any way resist.

One should readily understand the meaning of 'benefits the Ten Thousand Things.' There is no living thing in this world that could continue living without water. Water is a basis of life and is, beginning with humans, vital to all living organisms. Not only does water get used for the benefit of all things, but it also never resists, yielding perfectly to match whatever square, round, or other shaped container it may be poured into.

Water does not seek to remain always in high places, and moves itself, instead, lower and lower, always toward the lowest possible ground. It moves, in other words, in the direction 'despised by most,' towards that which is disliked by people, toward the lowest of positions. This form of water is, on the other hand, actually very close to the Way, and to the Spirit of the Universal God.

The passage which follows goes on to describe how people of this world possessing hearts similar to water would, in turn, behave:

*Land, when right, is a Residence*
*Deep, when right, is a Heart*
*Virtue, when right, is Giving*
*Belief, when right, is the Word*
*Order, when right, is Rule*
*Talent, when right, is Affairs*
*Time, when right, is Movement*
*Only this does not struggle—*
*It is, thus, never at blame.*

To say 'Land, when right, is a Residence' means to aspire to be the kind of person who improves everything around oneself. Just like the water that moistens the ground around it, this kind of person naturally makes others better, regardless of place or position.

The word 'deep' in 'Deep, when right' is often used in Chinese to express the timeless or eternal nature of things. It is included here to depict the deep, lucid, and permanent spirit Lao Tsu represents.

The single term 'virtue' found in the passage 'Virtue, when right' is meant to include all that is good. Explaining this with more Japanese adjectives, this virtue encompasses selfless love, forgiveness, mercy, and acts of wisdom. This word 'virtue' is used to describe a total—a complete—person. This is why 'Virtue, when right, is Giving' is said of those who possess a virtuous heart desiring to interact with others.

'Belief, when right, is the Word' means that words should always be words of truth—words that can be trusted—and should never be false. These are not words that tell falsehoods but are instead the honest kind of words that assure people with the feeling that 'If that is what he says, everything is all right.' These are words that are in harmony with the Way.

The word for 'believe' (信) in Japanese is written by placing the character for 'person' (人)[14] next to the character for 'word' (言). Belief, thus, literally means 'the words of a person.'

The character for 'person,' in turn, means the place where the spirit (霊 hi) comes to rest. This is a stopover for the Sun 日 (光 light), and represents the divine spiritual vibrations that have halted at, and are working within, a particular being. It is common practice today to interchangeably use the compound for 'human' (人間 ningen) and the character that depicts the 'true person' (人 hito), but the 'beings' referred to by these two terms are not, strictly speaking, the same. The term hito is the word that has been attached to the phenomenon of the divine spiritual vibrations as they work within this world. The term ningen, on the other hand, is the name that has been attached to the composite being that not only contains divine spiritual wavelengths (光 light), but that possesses karmic thought wavelengths (迷 illusion) as well. This is why the more one is purified, the truer a person (人) one becomes. It was to differentiate between these various realms of people that Shakyamuni adopted such names as 'Celestial Being,' 'Human,' 'Ashura,' and so on.

Belief, therefore, means the words of the true person. These words (言 *kotoba*) do not simply refer to those words that come out when the voice is emitted, but also include the vibrations of the thought waves themselves. Thus, when the 'true person's words' reverberate out into the branches, we have what are, in Japanese, termed 言葉 (*kotoba* 'word-leaves') that is, words. This term *kotoba* is thus made into the character 信 which, in turn, refers to the 'words (言) of the true person,' which are the waves emanating from the divine spirit itself. This is why the term 'belief' is so important, and, as Lao Tsu says, it has to gradually be communicated to people via good words.

'Order, when right, is Rule.' It goes without saying that order must be well established if there is to be government. The job of establishing such order has, even in Lao Tsu's day, been an extremely difficult one. Just because someone is later proclaimed to be a famous politician, for example, one cannot presume that the person enjoyed the same degree of fame during their time in office.

A politician should in no way be selfish, and must always be at one with the voice of Heaven—at one with the Spirit of God—if he or she is to establish order and effective rule. A person who cannot act in accordance with the Way cannot, as Lao Tsu says, conduct true politics.

If we were to apply this principle in examining the political figures of the world today, I wonder how many would actually meet Lao Tsu's standards. If a country's political leaders were to completely rid themselves of selfish interests and govern from the Spirit of God alone, their country would indeed enjoy peace and prosperity. Given the complexity of the world situation today, however, even the extremely gifted are thwarted by all manner of thought waves emanating from all over the world. To rule by order of the Spirit of God is no easy task.

By comparison, it is relatively easy for an individual to become selfless and, depending on the degree of one's efforts, it is possible for an individual to act out of the Spirit of God. As it is probably more difficult to realize this Spirit of God in politics than in any other field, I believe it is best to leave the issue of good politics to a not-too-distant future generation. It is still too early to put Lao Tsu's words into practice in the political realm.

'Talent, when right, is Affairs' means that when making something, one has to fully utilize one's abilities and avoid wastefulness. If one conducts oneself so as to fully develop one's talent, everyone will treat one well. When one works to the best of one's ability, one will naturally be granted important positions without any boasting or self-advertisement. What Lao Tsu seeks to emphasize here is the importance of always focusing on developing the Way, and upon nurturing the strengths of the Way.

'Time, when right, is Movement.' Regardless of how one flutters about, all will be for naught unless one's efforts are timed properly. Even the most able of persons have to wait for the right moment to express their talents, and those who do not know the importance of timing only endanger themselves. For example, had the prayer for world peace been recited during Honen[15] or Shinran's[16] time or during the Sengoku (Warring States) Era, not only would the prayer have been totally ineffective, but the person reciting it would probably have been considered crazy, perhaps even executed as a witch or sorcerer.

No task can be completed without properly balancing people, time, and place. Thus, while there may have been numerous saints and brilliant figures in the past, humanity still remains essentially unawakened. One is forced to conclude that it is because time and place were not matched that a fundamental awakening of humankind has not yet been realized.

The future of the people of this planet is now at stake, and we are today in a true life-or-death situation. Be totally obliterated or enter the way to a complete spiritual awakening—we have been brought to these two extremes. This is why the harmonious balancing of the three (people, place and time) will certainly be achieved soon. God is Love, and would not stand by idly watching as the people of this planet slide into the abyss of destruction. We are now at the very point where humanity on Earth can no longer survive without experiencing a true awakening.

We come next to the concluding lines, 'Only this does not struggle—It is, thus, never at blame.' Just as water does not struggle and is without blame, so, too, does a person who has become free from all competitive thoughts live with a peaceful spirit which, in turn, gives birth to actions free from blame or error.

A person who holds even the slightest competitive intentions is not capable of leading the kind of life that Lao Tsu speaks of in this chapter; such persons cannot be termed true pacifists. The self marks the origin as well as the terminus of the journey towards the making of a complete person. The self must be rooted in a peaceful spirit. Rooted firmly in this peaceful heart, spiritual riches accumulate naturally. The person who is not rooted in this peaceful spirit may, of course, accumulate spiritual riches, however, those riches may easily crumble. This is why it is essential that people nurture peaceful spirits and strive to shed any competitive feelings.

There are many instances where, because one believes one's own actions are correct while those of others are wrong, one then concludes that it is only natural to become angry at others. When viewed from the perspective of someone like myself who understands the past karma of individuals, there are, on the other hand, many instances where, even though in a particular instance one person might be correct and the other 100% wrong, if one factors in the various activities of both individuals in past worlds, the person who thinks himself right has actually committed many previous wrongs. This means there is more than sufficient reason for others to treat him 'wrongly.'

Whether we take individuals interacting with one another or disputes between entire peoples and nations, we cannot simply look at the particular circumstances of that time and place, but must consider instead the many historical and karmic factors out of which today's dispute is born. We cannot say that what is right at present is right overall, or that what is wrong today is wrong overall.

The same applies to various causes and 'isms.' The same cause or 'ism' that on the surface seems only to be fouling a country or disrupting its people may in fact be the dust aroused by a thorough cleansing of the karmic thoughts from the same.

For some reason, it seems to be necessary for humans to be cleansed from time to time in order for them to show their true form as God's children. The result of this is the many, admittedly, very odd-looking thought systems or movements at present. These are, in fact, necessary to help purge humanity of the many layers of karmic thoughts which have built up over time. One might think that people with proper spirits should become annoyed with these types of mistaken beliefs and movements. Yet when people become upset or competitive over such things, it only means that they, themselves, have departed from the Spirit of God.

This is why I suggest that people begin by placing all of their thoughts in a prayer for world peace, letting their thoughts and actions be renewed and corrected therein, and then lead their lives accordingly. There is nothing more essential to the all-important development of a peaceful spirit than to root one's life in prayer for world peace. Even the teachings of Lao Tsu that, on first glance, appear so difficult can be put into practice with surprising ease when they come from within regular practice of the world peace prayer.

*Kuu* (空)
Calligraphy by Masahisa Goi

# Chapter 7

# PRACTICE THE VOID
# IN THE EXTREME

*Practice the Void in the extreme*
  *and silence will be earnestly defended.*
*The Ten Thousand Things rise together*
  *while one watches them revert.*
*Everything flourishes yet each returns to the root.*
*To return to the root is called Silence.*
*This is called the return to Life.*
*The return to Life is called the Normal.*
*To know the Normal is called Bright.*
*When the Normal is not known*
  *disorder is made, and there is Evil.*
*If the Normal is known, one can receive.*
*To be able to receive is to be Public and to be Public is to be King.*
*To be King is to be Heaven and to be Heaven is to be The Way.*
*To be The Way is to be lasting.*
*Immerse the body fully and there is no danger.*

*Dôtokukyô, Chapter 16*

*Practice the Void in the extreme*

*and silence will be earnestly defended.*

As used commonly, the word Void (虚 *kyo*) means empty, and is used to write such things as 虚言 (empty words, i.e., falsehoods), 虚栄 (empty wealth, i.e., embellishment, ornamentation), 虚色 (empty color, i.e., affectations), or 虚無 (empty nothing, i.e., nothingness, nil). This character Void (虚) is therefore used to express all that is empty, all that is hollow, all that is lacking substance. For the same reason it is easy to misinterpret this word as representing the dishonest or untrue. A proper reading of this character is quite different.

The true meaning of 虚 (Void), while including the empty and hollow, is essentially the same as 空 (*Kuu*, emptiness) in that it means to empty oneself of all human thoughts of self-interest and limited wisdom. The realm of Emptiness (*Kuu* 空) is, however, truly inconceivable and may not be described by words. The term Void as used by Lao Tsu in 'Practice the Void in the extreme,' on the other hand, implies the existence of some level—some stage—at the state of *Kyo*. One feels at one with what is more commonly called the state of *Kuu* when one has reached the extreme of emptying oneself, and I think that it would not be incorrect to restate this opening line as 'Practice the Void (虚) in the extreme and become Empty (空)."

The outcome of this deliberation over terminology really does not matter much but, as most readers' doubts are not so easily removed, I have chosen to include the above discussion nevertheless. As the Lao Tsu speaking from within my own heart says, *Kuu* is both shallow and deep, and it is, therefore, probably best to think of *Kyo* as being one with *Kuu*.

Moving on to explain the meaning of the complete passage 'Practice the Void in the extreme/and silence will be earnestly defended'—if one is completely emptied of all thoughts of self-interest and limited wisdom, one will enter a pure state of silence where, regardless of the surrounding happenings or events, thoughts cease to be aroused. One becomes, in other words, 'silence that will be earnestly defended.'

If one enters the realm of *Kyo*, truly eliminating the self and overcoming the self or feelings of profit and loss that are linked to the same, one will not be surprised or upset by anything. Such a person will exist 'protecting silence.'

*The Ten Thousand Things rise together*
  *while one watches them revert.*
*Everything flourishes yet each returns to the root.*

Just as the plants and trees shoot forth new buds, profligate, and flourish together in spring, so do the 'Ten Thousand Things,' subject to each of their individual natures, suddenly become manifest, grow, age and decay, finally returning their form to the original world. Regardless of how something may appear to be prospering for a time in the visible world, everything has to return to its origin—the 'root'—of each self. The origin of the 'Ten Thousand Things' is, of course, contained within the Great Life Force; what is called the 'root' of each self is actually the resonance of the source of the life force that, in the case of a plant, manifests itself in this Earthly world as a plant. This is the Great Life Force that has been divided into the origin of all flora, fauna, and so on.

I do not think there are many who do not feel a sense of wonder when they stop to consider the process that goes on within each and every one of the tiny seeds that produce the magnificent and beautiful floral forms before us. The pulse of the plant's life that exists within the seed harmonizes with the vibrations of the Earth, and is then heightened to produce a splendid and beautiful form. The riches of this world are produced via the rhythms manifest in this world; these are, in turn, generated by the life force that is hidden within the self. This is, of course, not only true of flora, but applies to all things, animate and inanimate alike. Various vibrations of the life force also work to assist those rhythms in manifesting themselves in this world.

The above notwithstanding, Lao Tsu states that the riches of each individual must at some point once again be returned to their origin.

*To return to the root is called Silence.*
*This is called the return to Life.*
*The return to Life is called the Normal.*

Lao Tsu is saying that to return to the root, that is, to the original, is called 'Silence.' When Lao Tsu speaks of Silence, he means that there is not even the slightest thought of Self. There is, therefore, no movement separate from the origin. This is a realm devoid of thought waves. The original form of the Great Life Force as it begins to go into action as numerous life-waves is, in other words, 'Silence.'

When one enters this state of Silence, one has what is called *fuku-mei* (復命), 'the return to Life,' or 'union with the source of the living.' Lao Tsu then adds that this 'return to Life' is called the 'Normal.' 'Normal' as used by Lao Tsu is, however, completely different from the common sense 'normal' ordinarily used in this world. The word 'common' found in the expression 'common sense' does, on the other hand, actually stem from the true meaning of this word 'normal.' It has, however, come to mean that which is commonly known and can be confirmed by any ordinary person of this earthly world.

The 'normal' Lao Tsu speaks of describes the spiritual state of the original world that lies deep beneath the common sense of this world. For this reason, I expect the meaning of this will be difficult for most to grasp readily. The spirit that emanates from the state of *Kyo* is the spirit of the normal. Simply stated, 'Normal' is the condition in which life waves reverberate in perfect unison with the principles of the Universal Spirit as the spiritual expression of the Divine Heart of the Universal God.

*To know the Normal is called Bright.*
*When the Normal is not known*
  *disorder is made, and there is Evil.*
*If the Normal is known, one can receive.*

To know this state of the Normal is called Bright. Bright, as the word implies, means light and clear, that which is not dark, clouded, or confused. This is the Light that is the very heart of God Itself.

If the Normal is not known, one will think of and commit all kinds of disorderly acts and Evil will result. On this point, I always say that if one is capable of conducting one's own actions naturally as the spirit of God Itself, no acts of karmic thoughts will arise. As a result, there will no longer be any karmic waves to disturb the Self, inflict injury on others, damage the nation, or ruin the harmony of mankind.

As the words, 'If the Normal is known, one can receive' state, if one knows the Normal, one will become equal to the natural spirit, and will thus be capable of receiving—of being filled with—anything.

*To be able to receive is to be Public and to be Public is to be King.*
*To be King is to be Heaven and to be Heaven is to be The Way.*
*To be The Way is to be lasting.*
*Immerse the body fully and there is no danger.*

Everything from 'to be able to receive' to 'to be the Way' in this passage is used by Lao Tsu to describe the Spirit of God. Thus, if one can become one with this spirit, one will attain eternal life yet meet no danger or difficulty, although still in possession of a physical body.

Lao Tsu employs a variety of expressions—to be 'Public,' 'King,' 'Heaven,' or 'the Way.' He uses these, however, to point to the same state of 'extreme practice of the Void.' This is the spirit that has been completely made into *Kuu*, i.e., the Spiritual World of Divine Beings.

As an aside, the character 公 is used to mean 'public.' This word 'public' implies a wide-reaching vision that is completely devoid of self. The person whose self has been fully immersed within such a broad perspective is thus said to be a Public Figure.

There are few public figures on this planet who perform

their duties from this truly public position, however. Not only true today, this has been the case in previous ages as well. While perhaps not going as far as graft or corruption, most of those who serve as public figures do so from—and while emphasizing—their own self-centered positions. Beginning with the heads of the various ministries and moving on down through the many bureaucrats below, I do not think there are many who perform their duties with their selves fully immersed within the public perspective. There are, to be sure, plenty of people who conduct the work assigned to them with vigor. The true public figure is, however, quite different from this. Totally devoid of all selfish thoughts relating to lifestyle or position, one naturally enters the spiritual ground called the Public when one becomes *Kuu*.

While the public viewpoint is, indeed, profound, to teach such things to the people who hold public positions today is all but impossible. That is why I think it best, using my own terminology, to place the vanishing phenomena of one's selfish spirit within a spirit of prayer and go about one's job as usual. This spirit of prayer should, if possible, be expressed in totally public words such as those of the prayer for world peace.

Next, we come to the word 'King.' The character for King (王) is composed of an upper horizontal line that signifies Heaven and a lower horizontal line that signifies Earth.

Between these two, Heaven and Earth, is then found a cross (+) which is, in turn, the shape which supports and harmonizes Heaven and Earth.

Putting this in more simple terms, humans have to be able to harmonize the real within the ideal (this harmony is shown in the cross) and to fuse material problems with spiritual ones in order to express Heaven's ideals on Earth. The person possessing this ability is called 'King.' This person, therefore, has to be a divine being who makes the wisdom of God his or her own in order to become King. On the other hand, the world is thrown into disorder by those who become leaders only by birth or through lust for power, yet lack the ability to harmonize ideals with reality.

A person who practices 'the void in the extreme' can, in this way, become public, king, Heaven and the Way. Lao Tsu concludes by saying the physical body of such a person is secure as well.

The ancient teachings of wise people such as Lao Tsu or Confucius state that it is enough to simply enter such a condition or, in some cases, that it is essential that one enter this sort of mental state. The method for doing so, however, has not been written down. Even if such a method had been recorded, it would most probably not have been an easy one to perform in practice. Sages of this kind no doubt purified their disciples through the light of their own divine personalities, in order that they might naturally achieve their own paths. The same might not be readily achieved, however, using only the books and other records left for later genera-tions.

That is why it was necessary for someone to appear in a position such as my own in order to instruct people in a simple method for realizing the principles expounded by Lao Tsu and others. The method of Vanishing Phenomena via the Prayer for World Peace is that simple method.

# Chapter 8

# THAT WHICH IS BROKEN
# IS MADE ANEW

*If it can bend, it is all.*

*If bent, it can be straightened.*

*If empty, it can be filled.*

*If broken, it can be made anew.*

*If scarce, there is some.*

*If plentiful, one may wander.*

*The Sage that adheres to this embraces the One*

    *and becomes the model for all under heaven.*

*He does not show himself and is for that reason brilliant.*

*Does no right on his own and is for that reason clear.*

*Does not boast and is for that reason accomplished.*

*Is not conceited and for that reason endures.*

*Does not struggle*

    *and for that reason none under heaven struggle with him.*

*The ancient words 'If it can bend, it is all' are not empty.*

*We have only to return to this to truly become all.*

*Dôtokukyô, Chapter 22*

*If it can bend, it is all.*
*If bent, it can be straightened.*
*If empty, it can be filled.*
*If broken, it can be made anew.*
*If scarce, there is some.*
*If plentiful, one may wander.*

Lao Tsu begins this chapter with the words 'If it can bend, it is all. If bent, it can be straightened.' This chapter is often cited by those who believe Lao Tsu's teachings to be pessimistic, to illustrate how truly negative his philosophy is. I myself, though, have never pictured Lao Tsu as a pessimist of any sort.

Some, for example, explain the phrase 'If it can bend, it is all' by using the following negativist analogy: If a tree grows too straight, it will be cut and used for lumber. If the same tree were to grow in a bent shape, though, it would be unfit for use as lumber and would consequently be left to complete its life as a tree. Similarly, a person who extends oneself straight out into the world may be spotted as good material and put to use. The critics then conclude that Lao Tsu teaches that we should always be restrained, de-emphasize the self, and lead a safe, inconspicuous existence in order to protect ourselves and to avoid the troubles and pains of others who grow too 'straight.' I cannot accept an explanation such as this that depicts Lao Tsu to have been a prophet of this kind of pessimism.

Lao Tsu is not describing a negative way of protecting one's own self, or body, when he says 'If it can bend, it is all/If bent, it can be straightened,' but is, rather, here explaining the freedom of the spirit that is not attached to a single material object, position, or any other thing with shape or form. A free person is one who can 'bend' freely according to the situation or the people who face him or her. It is someone who can bow without clinging to the desire to show how great or right he or she is. (The 'bend' in 'If bent, it can be straightened' means to bend the body in Chinese.) Lao Tsu's words are always rooted in and teach the free and unrestricted nature of life; they are not words that simply preach how to protect oneself from the outside world.

The passages that follow all describe the state that is naturally born of this total freedom: 'If empty, it can be filled./If broken, it can be made anew./If scarce, there is some.' For Lao Tsu, the only thing that is important is to live according to the true Self, the mainstream of the Self that flows from the one, Great Life.

Lao Tsu warns us, however, to be extremely wary of excesses by stating 'If there is plenty, one may wander.' This is because, even in the case of the finest people, it is easy to lose sight of what is important when there is 'plenty.' This is as true for a surplus of academic knowledge as it is for a surplus of material objects.

Among these passages, the one I am most drawn to is that which reads 'If broken, it can be made anew.' These are truly fine words, and my own teaching of the constantly 'vanishing images' is actually a gentler, more easily practiced version of the same philosophy of 'breaking.'

The phenomenal world is a place in which old things are broken down and new ones are constantly being born. To cling forever to the old obstructs the birth of the new. Attachment thus impedes the natural movement of the universe. Even if the old is splendid and fine, it absolutely cannot remain just as it is. We must avoid attaching ourselves to the old forms of things.

According to the principles of cosmic science,[17] the cosmic particles (17 levels beyond the electrons, mesons, protons, and corpuscles just discernible by today's most advanced scientific techniques) that are the true corpuscles of the Universal Source are constantly being released from the heart of the universe while old cosmic particles, having once been utilized, are constantly being dispelled.

Some of these cosmic particles vibrate on a material wave length, while others vibrate on a spiritual wave length. Our world is constructed in accordance with the harmony of these two. Old material and spiritual particles are instantly replaced by their counterparts, and both are constantly in a process of metabolic change.

Even if we are uninformed about this principle and continue to cling to our old self and to material things, new cosmic particles are being sent one after the other from the heart of the universe in order that the old self and old material objects may disappear. These new particles cause continual metabolic change, irrespective of our preferences or individual abilities to adapt.

A state of continual extinguishing has arisen, whereby thought waves relating to old habits and attachments to old things and conditions are continuously broken down and extinguished in the form of sickness, misfortune, or, where nations are concerned, war.

This is what I have been explaining to people through the concept of 'vanishing images.' According to the principle of metabolic change, there is no need to fear being broken, destroyed, torn apart, or extinguished, because such things occur through the divine spirit that works to deepen and heighten each of us individually, and humanity as a whole, so that we can behave as true children of God, and turn this world into a divine world. It is the design of the universe that all humanity be born anew as people of truth—divine beings who do not inflict injury or destroy, and who are directly united with all other people within the infiniteness of Life itself. For this reason, God, taking the form of numerous divinities, is now sending forth a great light of rescue to this planet, carrying with it a tremendously powerful elixir of merciful love to help the people of this world.

'If broken, it can be made anew' is truly a fine passage. As outlined above, the method I employ originally grew out of a desire to lessen the impact people receive at these moments of 'breaking.' It teaches that all of the evil, misfortune, sickness, and discord of this world are the vanishing images of distorted thought waves. These are thoughts that have, in the past, wandered away from the divine spirit of God. If one abides by the principle of 'vanishing images,' the new, true person who is one's real Self will be born, along with other new people of truth. My method also teaches people to keep in mind the principle of 'vanishing images,' to pray for the harmony of humankind, and to plunge into the prayer for world peace, making it the basis of their daily life.

In this way, discrepancies between the old (i.e., karmic thought waves from past worlds) and the newly-born Self (the true, divine Self) are beautifully erased in a great, divine light; and the process of metabolic change—in ourselves and in humanity—moves towards completion with as little fear, injury, or pain as possible.

This is why there is no need to fear evil, misfortune, sickness or calamity. Everything is working toward the creation of improved conditions and the birth of a new and better person. Chisel this into your heart while continuing to pray the prayer for world peace, and the rest will take care of itself. Lao Tsu inside of me keeps repeating the words of truth in a loud voice, over and over again.

*The Sage that adheres to this embraces the One*
*and becomes the model for all under heaven.*
*He does not show himself*
*and is for that reason brilliant.*
*Does no right on his own*
*and is for that reason clear.*
*Does not boast*
*and is for that reason accomplished.*
*Is not conceited*
*and for that reason endures.*
*Does not struggle*
*and for that reason none under heaven struggle with him.*
*The ancient words 'If it can bend, it is all' are not empty.*
*We have only to return to this*
*to truly become all.*

The Sage is a person who 'embraces the One and becomes a model for all under Heaven.' He or she is, in short, an example for others to follow. The 'One' referred to here is the divine spirit of the Universal God. Once united with this One, there is no longer any need to show oneself off to the world, as there is no longer any self-centeredness. Unified with the divine spirit of the Universal God, the Sage leads a perfectly natural life that permits his or her own personal mission to be expressed unimpeded. Once having entered this state, the person shines brightly, like a mirror reflecting all that surrounds it.

There is even less of a need for thinking oneself right, self-approval or bragging, and the person ceases all struggles with others, while adding one accomplishment on top of another. If everyone were to become this kind of Sage, all strife would vanish from this planet.

As the ancients said, once one is able to be free, whether bent or straight, one can also complete the mission of one's life. If one becomes completely free, one will recognize that the word 'complete' is not false. All that human beings need to do is to achieve this free spirit and complete their missions, and then return their worldly body to the spirit of the Universal God.

This marks Lao Tsu's conclusion to this chapter. It is admittedly difficult to discern the true meaning of this passage from the original text alone. Generally speaking, if a person simply reads the words of someone like Lao Tsu—someone who manifests eternal life itself—the words will most likely be interpreted according to one's particular state of mind at the time of reading, not necessarily as Lao Tsu originally intended them. When presenting Lao Tsu, the interpreter's own degree of awakening is a matter of utmost importance.

When one stops to think that, even today, the monthly publication of my own articles and speeches are subject to a wide variety of interpretations according to the mood, of the reader—sometimes completely misconstrued in the process—I am certain most can appreciate just how difficult it is to accurately interpret the words left behind by someone as ancient as Lao Tsu.

Lao Tsu is inside me lending assistance as I write these lectures, saying to me such things as 'It doesn't matter how others are trying to interpret me—I don't remember ever saying anything like that.' I realize there are various other lectures on Lao Tsu available, but I hope you will read these with the assurance that they have been interpreted while being completely one with the spirit of Lao Tsu.

Being one with the spirit of Lao Tsu does not mean that I have any less respect for him, however. While writing these lectures I have, in fact, felt constantly humbled by the tremendous breadth and scope of this person. Lao Tsu is a divine person who far transcends relativistic terms such as 'great' or 'not great,' and it is this great Sage 'who does not struggle,' Lao Tsu, who instills me with his life force which continues to lead me on my way.

Lao Tsu is alive today. He is the indispensable force, the rich life blood, that flows throughout my prayer for world peace, supporting it with Christ and Shakamuni as well. I have every confidence that the prayer for world peace will continue to grow rapidly.

# Chapter 9

# BECOME THE SAME IN LOSS AS THE PERSON OF LOSS

*Unusual Words are Natural.*

*Thus the whirlwind does not outlast the morning,*
*    nor does the thunderstorm outlive the day.*

*What makes them?*

*Heaven and Earth.*

*Yet, even Heaven and Earth are incapable of lasting.*

*What, then, about people?*

*The person who follows The Way is the same in The Way as the*
*    person of The Way, the same in Virtue as the person of Virtue,*
*    the same in Loss as the person of Loss.*

*If you become the same in The Way as the person of The Way,*
*    he, too, will take joy in your obtaining The Way.*

*If you become the same in Virtue as the person of Virtue,*
*    he, too, will take joy in your obtaining Virtue.*

*If you become the same in Loss as the person of Loss,*
*    he, too, will take joy in your obtaining Loss.*

*Not enough belief is disbelief.*

*Dôtokukyô, Chapter 23*

*Unusual Words are Natural.*

*Thus the whirlwind does not outlast the morning,*

  *nor does the thunderstorm outlive the day.*

*What makes them?*

*Heaven and Earth.*

*Yet, even Heaven and Earth are incapable of lasting.*

The meaning of 'Unusual Words' in the opening line of this chapter is, just as the Chinese characters show: strange, or unique (希) words (言). Put another way, 'Unusual Words' are words that do not show on the surface, words that cannot be made to show on the surface, or words that do not exist and that are not words at all.

A form that does not show itself and is not clearly manifest on the surface is called 'Natural.' That form may show itself violently at times in the shape of a whirlwind, gale, or thunderstorm. Rarely, though, will the winds continue to blow all night or the rains pour for more than a few days at a time.

What is it that makes these winds blow or these rains fall? Heaven and Earth. Yet even that which is driven by the vast and seemingly unlimited power of Heaven and Earth will not last long if it continues to manifest itself in the extreme manner of a thunderstorm, gale, or other natural phenomenon.

The main point of this passage is that even Heaven and Earth do not constantly show themselves fully in this manner. In the following lines, Lao Tsu then moves on to discuss a more lasting method of expression.

*The person who follows The Way is the same*
*in The Way as the person of The Way,*
*the same in Virtue as the person of Virtue,*
*the same in Loss as the person of Loss.*
*If you become the same in The Way as the person of The Way,*
*he, too, will take joy in your obtaining The Way.*
*If you become the same in Virtue as the person of Virtue,*
*he, too, will take joy in your obtaining Virtue.*
*If you become the same in Loss as the person of Loss,*
*he, too, will take joy in your obtaining Loss.*
*Not enough belief is disbelief.*

This section may be summarized as follows: As even Heaven and Earth are incapable of sustaining an extreme method of expression for an extended period, how much less possible will it be to ensure the harmony of this world if human beings show themselves in a similarly violent manner.

Moving next to the question of what should be done, Lao Tsu says that those of the Way should be the same as the Way itself. One has to be equal in the Way with those who practice the proper way of life and have climbed aboard the Spirit of the Universal God. One must lead the same sort of life oneself or, as Lao Tsu says in the next line, one has to be equal in spirit to the person of Virtue—be 'the same in Virtue as the person of Virtue.'

As we have already seen in other chapters, Lao Tsu's method is to frankly state the most difficult of things out-right. Even though one may nod and receive these teachings with one's intellect, Lao Tsu's words may not be realized in practice by most. One has to be of the same high state—'the same in the Way as the person of the Way'—as the true person of the Way and, while one may think one is capable of facing up to such a spirit with the same sort of spirit oneself, it is most probable that one will be unable to handle a person who treads a higher spiritual path with such a singular mind.

Lao Tsu's teachings are, as I have frequently pointed out, intended for sages and saints of a similarly high spiritual state.

Even though the souls of those who are not of the same spiritual condition as such sages or saints may feel soothed by these lessons, realistically speaking I think it is impossible for such persons to put Lao Tsu's teachings into practice.

On the other hand, while it may not be possible for the average person to go as far as Lao Tsu's realm per se, it certainly is possible for anyone to discover the Way that he points to and to take the first one or two steps. This is why I think it acceptable for people to simply imitate Lao Tsu's Way, and to follow in the direction of his guiding finger—even if only one step at a time—with a feeling of thanks for being allowed to walk the Way of Truth. This is certainly better than giving up at the start, saying that one can't possibly tread such a path.

The human spirit is an interesting thing indeed. Once one has made up one's mind and begins something, many things previously thought impossible are accomplished with surprising ease. With tireless practice of sports, for example, people become quite advanced in those particular ways, and change completely from when they first started upon that path almost before they know it. This catharsis is, however, first and foremost a question of spirit. After a few months or years of constant spiritual training and continued polishing, people will one day realize what fine human beings they have become.

There are many examples among people of my acquaintance who have entered a noticeably different state through the continual practice of a single spiritual training method: the prayer for world peace. This is why Lao Tsu says we become 'the same in the Way' if we listen attentively and with sincerity to a teacher who is particularly advanced in the Way. Thus, by saying 'become the same in Virtue' Lao Tsu means that the person of virtue will be pleased by and, in turn, love the person who feels love and respect for his lofty virtue. Not only for such persons of virtue, but for all of us, it is natural to be pleased by those who listen to our words attentively and to feel oneness with them as kindred spirits in the Way.

A sincere heart is the most important factor for becoming loved and respected by others. People with sincere hearts can harmonize with anyone, naturally blend with the Way and accumulate virtue. The only thing that is responsible for delivering me to my present realm, for example, is not that I have a particularly good head on my shoulders or that I am otherwise gifted. The one truly indispensable factor to my own spiritual development is my sincere heart. A sincere heart is difficult to come by, yet is vital to mastering the Way. God is pleased most by people with sincere hearts.

'If you become the same in Loss...he, too, will take joy in your obtaining Loss.' Most people probably think it easier to face people who have lost, are paupers or are ill (the so-called despondent types) than it is to face 'the person of the Way' or 'the person of Virtue' (the great and outstanding) discussed above, but such is not the case.

Nothing is more difficult than having to deal with people who have problems or who have lost hope. A sincere heart will not here alone suffice, and in such cases it is necessary to possess keen powers of perception in order to see into the other's spiritual condition so that one may then join with it. A deep heart of love is required in dealing with those who 'have lost.'

The basic problem, then, is how to nurture such powers of observation and perception, and how to develop a deep, loving heart of one's own. A person who is simply good and sincere might easily end up thinking the same disgruntled thoughts as the person who is complaining, and might be pulled down by stories of other people's misfortunes. People might find some sense of relief in complaining or fulminating but in time this habit of complaining takes root and, without even being aware of the weakness that caused them to fall into despair, they choose a way of life that hampers further uplifting of their spirit.

The bitter complaints of these people might, if repeated over and over again, eventually engulf the good and sincere individual within its karmic waves, disrupt the individual's life and spiritual condition, and spell the ruin of Lao Tsu's teaching of truth, 'become the same in Loss.' It is, just as Lao Tsu states, good to place oneself in the position of the other in order to comfort and strengthen them; one must do so, however, by melting into the heart of the other while at the same time taking care not to be pulled into their karmic thoughts.

To be 'the same in Loss' it is thus necessary to place oneself in the position of one's own Guardian Spirit and original divine spirit. This position of the original divine spirit lies within the heart of God, and here, too, exist all love, wisdom and strength. Words spoken from this standpoint of the original spirit will naturally comfort and encourage others. Cleansing waves of light will travel from oneself to lift away the layers of karmic thoughts from others without allowing oneself to become enveloped in those same waves of illusory thoughts.

We come next to the question of how to go about placing ourselves in the position of the original divine spirit. This is done via the steadfast spirit of prayer. It is best if this spirit of prayer is large enough to include the well-being of others, as well as peace for humanity—an all-inclusive prayer, such as the prayer for world peace. Moreover, a prayer for the peace of humanity also possesses a unique power born from the resonance of deep love, that wishes for the accomplishment of other people's heavenly missions as well as one's own.

Even if one were able to lighten another person's present grief or adversity, that alone would not do much to help the person accomplish the mission of his or her life. Rather, the important thing is to have a deep, loving heart that holds a more fundamental aim: for the other person to fulfill their divine mission and to complete their life in this world as a person of truth, so that the person's future work, to be undertaken in the next world, can be made easier for them.

This kind of deep, loving heart does not become enveloped by karmic thought waves, however strong they might be. Only such a deep, loving heart will continue shining brightly, despite the presence of karmic thoughts coming from people around oneself.

It does not do oneself or others any good only to regard despairing people with pity. And, just as Lao Tsu says in closing ('not enough belief is disbelief'), we have to believe in the heavenly missions of others and realize that all people were born into this world possessing their own unique and individual missions. 'Belief' means to have faith in the great, divine love of the Universe and in the fulfillment of the missions of others.

*Chapter 10*

# INDEPENDENT OF IT THERE IS NO CHANGE WHEREVER IT IS PRACTICED THERE IS NO DANGER

*That which is mixed is born before Heaven and Earth.*

*It is silent and sublime.*

*Independent of it there is no change,*

*Wherever it is practiced there is no danger.*

*One should make it the mother of all under Heaven.*

*Yet, I know not its name.*

*By its nickname, it is called The Way.*

*One could, likewise, name it 'The Great.'*

*The Great is called departure, the departure is called*
*    distance, and the distant is called return.*

*Thus, The Way is Great.*

*Heaven is Great, Earth is Great, and the King is Great.*

*The Four-Greats exist in the world*
*    and the King is included as one of these.*

*Man follows Earth, Earth follows Heaven,*

*Heaven follows Way, and Way follows Nature.*

*Dôtokukyô, Chapter 25*

*That which is mixed is born before Heaven and Earth.*
*It is silent and sublime.*
*Independent of it there is no change,*
*Wherever it is practiced there is no danger.*
*One should make it the mother of all under Heaven.*

It seems clear that 'That which is mixed' is not a material object such as is found in this world. To describe this in any further detail is indeed a difficult task. In short, the fundamental 'something' that precedes both Heaven and Earth, 'That which is mixed,' might most simply be called the Universal God.

Rather than seek another name to describe the same thing, one could of course simply skip over this section and proceed to the next. I think it is easier, however, for the intellectual or knowledge-seeking person to understand the fundamental existence of the Spirit of the Universal God through the addition of a variety of explanations instead. Considering that Lao Tsu himself employed a number of different terms to express this fundamental entity (Omniscient/Omnipotent), there certainly is an incentive for me to continue his work in these chapters on Lao Tsu and elsewhere.

That which precedes both Heaven and Earth is, as the words 'silent' and 'sublime' suggest, without sound, shape or form. Existing in this way, everything is included within it; hence, it is said to be that which is 'mixed.' It does not rely on anyone or anything, and it remains an absolute one, even when thoughts of calling on others arise. Because this exists prior to Heaven and Earth, nothing exists separate from it. It is entirely independent and self-reliant. Furthermore it will meet no danger and commit no errors, regardless of how it acts or how it chooses to proceed. Lao Tsu calls this the parent who gives birth to all under Heaven. It is the 'mother of all under Heaven.'

Put into more modern terms, this would probably best be termed the Creator, Maker or Absolute. It is this that Lao Tsu then tries to express using a variety of different expressions in the section that follows.

Of the many expressions used by Lao Tsu in this chapter, I am particularly drawn by the words, 'Wherever it is practiced there is no danger.' This single phrase coincides with the Philosophy of Light which I espouse, and it reaffirms for me the correctness of this principle.

That which is born before the Heaven and Earth is the mother of all under Heaven. This omnipotent power 'travels without danger.' No matter where it wanders or how it chooses to go, nothing threatens it and there are no mishaps. One has to conclude that the people and rest of creation born of an omnipotent power that knows no dangers or errors must themselves be intrinsically perfect beings that are likewise devoid of dangers and errors. Lao Tsu is here clearly pointing to the way of bright thought—my Philosophy of Light.

This is why, regardless of how evil or full of misery and wrong the world may appear, I continue to reject the existence of any such negative forces, saying instead that these are merely indications that the Universal Divine Spirit has not yet fully shown itself—forms that will vanish once the spirit and light of the Universal God are made clearly evident. This is also the reason why I explain that all thoughts and actions of evil, hardship, or wrong are vanishing phenomena, and that, once they have vanished, the light of the original divine spirit will shine forth clearly.

*Yet, I know not its name.*

*By its nickname, it is called The Way.*

*One could, likewise, name it 'The Great.'*

*The Great is called departure, the departure is called distance,*
    *and the distant is called return.*

*Thus, The Way is Great.*

*Heaven is Great, Earth is Great, and the King is Great.*

*The Four-Greats exist in the world*
    *and the King is included as one of these.*

*Man follows Earth, Earth follows Heaven,*

*Heaven follows The Way, and The Way follows Nature.*

In this passage Lao Tsu states that he himself does not know the name of that which precedes and is born before Heaven and Earth. If, however, he were to give it a name, Lao Tsu continues to say that he would dub it 'the Way,' or, going one step further, 'The Great.'

This absolute being precedes everything and, as all life exists within it, all of the activities of living organisms are conducted inside it as well. For this reason, human beings— as individual strands of the Great Life Force—tend to gaze up at the Absolute Being, since it should be possible to bring themselves into direct contact with it by tracing their life to its origin and source. Try as they will, however, they never seem able to touch the innermost part of the Absolute Being. This is because they still retain their individual consciousness of self. Try as they may to locate the heart of the Absolute Being, for as long as their consciosness resides within their individual life force, they can only comprehend that which exists in the realm of the individual self. The realm of the Great Life Force—the Absolute Being—thus remains a mystery.

In response to this, Lao Tsu teaches that we should always act out of No-action (*Mu-i*), and lead lives that surpass the consciousness of self. Lao Tsu is himself a person who acts in No-action and who has penetrated deep within the heart of the Absolute Being (Great Life Force). This notwithstanding, even Lao Tsu concedes that he does not know the true name of the Absolute.

All names that have been attached to the Absolute are titles assigned to it by human beings. At present, it is most common to use the terms God, *Nyorai*, or Buddha, but Lao Tsu used the name Way (道). He also used the names Great (大), Depart (逝), Distant (遠), and Return (反). All of these titles are applied to describe the Absolute and thus mean virtually the same thing.

One can, for example, explain the character for Great (大) in the following manner: the single horizontal line (一) represents the oneness that precedes the distinction between Heaven and Earth and holds within it the unity of Heaven and Earth. Atop this 'one' (一) is then placed a person (人), to form the complete character (大), Great. A person, as is frequently pointed out in these essays, is the place where the spirit comes to rest and is where Yin and Yang are unified.

Describing this a bit further, Great is the state where everything comes to a stop in perfect equilibrium. The person placed atop the One (一) that exists prior to the division of oneness into Heaven and Earth is not therefore a person who possesses a physical body of any kind but is rather the fundamental person (人 Hito, 霊止) instead. This is not only the place where the 'spirit stops' (霊止) or a 'spiritual person' (霊人), but is also a person positioned above the One that precedes the division into Heaven and Earth.

Put in more modern terminology, the Great Person represents the figure of the Universal God. Stated in its simplest, yet most accurate written form, this Universal God may best be expressed by the character 大 (*Dai* Big, Great). This form of expression is typical of Lao Tsu's grand nature.

Once set into motion, this Great (大) becomes a Departure (逝 *Sei*), Distant (遠 *En*), or a Return (反 *Han*). For this reason, Lao Tsu says the Way is Great, Heaven is Great, Earth is Great, and, finally, that the King is Great. The Way, Heaven, Earth and King are all Great because they are manifestations of the Universal God. Lao Tsu concludes by stating 'The Four-Greats exist in the world, and the King is included as one of these' and that Man, Earth, Heaven, the Way, and Nature each follow, and each is in harmony with what precedes it.

Lao Tsu says that Man, Heaven, Earth, and the Way are significant parts of this Great—that is to say, they are significant manifestations of the Universal God—and that human beings, in particular, stand as one of the four great manifestations of the Universal God.

Human beings, he continues, are subject to Earth. Without going into detail, suffice it to say that to 'follow Earth' means to be sustained in accordance with the laws of Earth. Earth, Heaven, the Way and Nature, likewise exist in accordance with the laws that apply to their own relative positions. Each follows the laws that apply to it and prosper together as manifestations of the Spirit of the Universal God.

This Spirit of the Universal God gives birth to, nurtures, and envelops all. It is what drives the life force inside of everything in existence.

Explaining this in terms of cosmic science, this Spirit of the Universal God is the birthplace—the nucleus—of everything in the universe. It is, likewise, the origin of the Universal Particles that work within all objects—animate or inanimate—that serve as the source of everything in creation and that sustain all activity. These Universal Particles may be divided into two types, Spiritual and Material. Everything is created, sustained, and altered by the various combinations or separations of these particles.

Thus, while the Spirit of the Universal God envelops and surrounds everything, it also exists within all. As all worlds consist of activities of the Spirit (Heart) of the Universal God, we are left to conclude that the single truly fundamental existence is that of the Universal God Itself.

An individual who receives life and lives on this planet does not, therefore, merely live as the physical form of what is usually called a 'person;' he or she exists instead as all of creation living in the form of one person.

To express this in simple terms, for a human being to be born in this world, there must first be a mother and a father. Once born, it is then necessary that some form of nourishment be supplied, via the parents, to this child. Where does this sustenance—essential to the physical body and life—

that flows via the parents come from? It comes from Nature, from various manifestations of the Spirit of the Universal God.

Knowledge of this is essential in order for a human being to develop into a True Person. If one overlooks this fundamental principle, one cannot live as a full-fledged 'stopping place of the Spirit' (霊止 *Hito*), who realizes that he or she exists as a branching out of Divine Life itself.

Without a basic feeling of gratitude for the blessings of universal divine love, and for the gifts received from everything in creation, one cannot fulfill one's role as a governing spirit of creation, one of the Four Greats, or a True Person. This applies regardless of how great an individual's worldly knowledge might be. On the contrary, a lifestyle rooted only in this kind of 'knowledge' will eventually bring about the ruin of the individual, which in turn will contribute to the destruction of humanity as well.

The essence of this human karma was clearly expressed with the announcement made by one of the large nations that it has developed a rocket which may be launched from a satellite circling our planet and which can hit any target at will. My first reaction upon learning this news was that there is nothing more frightening than knowledge in the hands of fools who know nothing at all about the fundamental nature of human beings.

Unless the people of this planet make efforts toward

knowing what a human being really is, they will end up destroying themselves. It is to eliminate this kind of absurdity that I write these essays, practice the prayer for world peace, and strive to let more and more people know about it.

*Chapter 11*

# NOTHING IS ABANDONED
# NOTHING IS DISCARDED

*The good deed leaves no tracks, the good word no trace*

*and good measure does not use calculated plans.*

*The gate well shut has no lock,*

*yet may not be opened;*

*The good knot is tied not with twine,*

*yet may not be undone.*

*The Sage who holds to this always saves people well.*

*Thus no one is abandoned.*

*This always saves things well.*

*Thus nothing is discarded.*

*(This is called Strike Bright.)*

*Thus, the good person is the not-good's teacher,*

*and the not-good person is the good's resource.*

*He who does not value this teacher or who does not love*

*that resource may have wisdom, yet will wander greatly.*

*Dôtokukyô, Chapter 27*

*The good deed leaves no tracks, the good word no trace*
  *and good measure does not use calculated plans.*
*The gate well shut has no lock,*
  *yet may not be opened;*
*The good knot is tied not with twine,*
  *yet may not be undone.*

Just as the cart is not stopped by its tracks while moving along the path, so too is the spirit of the person who performs a truly good deed not halted by self-pride. Nor are his or her actions given wide or glorious recognition in the eyes of others.

Truly good words, likewise, do not damage or in any way cause injury to oneself or others. Regardless of how splendid the words of a Sage may be, when mentioned to others they will be of no benefit if the other party happens to be busy with other things, in a dark mood, or simply not inclined towards such talk at that particular moment. Such ill-timed discussions not only bring others no benefit, but frequently result in injury on both sides. Comments intended to help only worsen the other's mood and, as a result of the other party's thoughts directed against oneself, one's own heart begins to cloud over. This is why one must wait for the right person and time before speaking even the best of words. In addition to person and time, the final thing to observe before speaking is place as well.

The passage 'good measure does not use calculated plans' means that the best calculations are not made by pushing the beads of an abacus one by one, but rather require that one go beyond immediate thoughts of profit or loss, see deep into things, and grasp their general outline. Not limited to mathematical calculations, the principle of ascertaining the basics first and of looking past the secondary issue of weighing profit or loss applies to all manner of planning as well. The plan or computation that stems from this kind of profound spirit is termed 'the good plan' by Lao Tsu.

The next line, 'The gate well shut has no lock, yet may not be opened' means that people's hearts are just like a well-sealed door that uses no bars or locks, yet cannot be opened. All that one needs to do is to unite one's own heart with the principles of the Universe (the heart of God) and one will be freed from all injury. Even without being on constant guard by hiding one's true feelings, fleeing from people one finds disagreeable, or always keeping one's heart under lock and key, evil thoughts will no longer be there for others to observe.

Finally, we come to the passage 'The good knot is tied not with twine, yet may not be undone.' Lao Tsu says here that true union is very different from something that has been wrapped with twine or constricted by all manner of detailed clauses. On the contrary, true union is a complete and total exchange between two hearts. Only such a bond will remain fast in face of strife or conflict of interests, despite the absence of restricting ties, pledges, or contractual clauses. The union of two hearts is a far more fundamental kind of bond.

The lifestyle Lao Tsu speaks of here is truly profound, and is nothing short of exquisite.

*The Sage who holds to this always saves people well.*
*Thus no one is abandoned.*
*This always saves things well.*
*Thus nothing is discarded.*
*(This is called Strike Bright.)*
*Thus, the good person is the not-good's teacher,*
*  and the not-good person is the good's resource.*
*He who does not value this teacher or who does not love*
*  that resource may have wisdom, yet will wander greatly.*

As the Sage is one who leads the life described in the previous section, he or she is 'good' and thus capable of saving others. This is why Lao Tsu says none are abandoned.

The difficulty of realizing this teaching in practice, however, is virtually unrivaled. I myself have had significant first-hand experience with the difficulties of helping all manner of disagreeable, wretched, and so-called corrupt people without deserting them. One might even say that I have had so much experience with such people that I have had enough.

Most will not, of course, turn their backs on close relatives or acquaintances that, for some karmic reason, they are obligated to assist, even if these persons are of a disagreeable disposition, insane, or simply malicious. If there are not close relationships binding the two, however, most tend to abandon such individuals because they are just too much trouble.

Lao Tsu says that a Sage, on the other hand, will lend assistance to such people without turning his back, even though he could easily separate himself from them if he wanted to. The Sage aids these individuals despite the obstacles presented to his own freedom of movement.

If one stops to consider oneself lending assistance to everybody and anybody that comes seeking, I think most cannot help but be impressed with the dignity of the love of someone capable of so doing. Performing a true action of love is no easy matter, unlike the usual kindness rendered with the thought, 'I'll lend him a hand because he's a good guy in trouble' or 'I'll help her out because she likes me,' and so on.

An example of the quality of action worthy of the Sage Lao Tsu is describing may be found in Victor Hugo's novel, *Les Miserables*. I think the section that depicts the bishop

Myriel protecting Jean Valjean from the authorities even after he has attempted to kill the bishop and make off with the silver candlesticks—and in the end sending him on his way with the stolen candlesticks still in his possession—is the kind of action typical of the Sage Lao Tsu speaks of. How does one become a person who performs such actions? Only by entering the deep state of *Kuu* and becoming the person of No-action whom Lao Tsu describes.

On the other hand, entering the deep state of *Kuu* or *Mu-i* is not easily accomplished. Moreover, I cannot think of anything more misdirected than for people to pride and praise themselves for having done something to help another or for performing minor actions of love. The person who does not abandon others and who does not 'discard things' does not carry out actions of love or relief consciously, thinking to accomplish a particular end. Nor is this the kind of person who, reflecting on the depth of his own love, then decides to stop performing acts of love because he has already done enough for others.

Acts that stem from the bottom of *Mu-i* and that come from the depths of Emptiness express themselves perfectly naturally as acts of love and redemption. This is why Lao Tsu states that the Sage's heart is not halted by thoughts of his love for people, or by thoughts of having just uplifted someone. His thoughts flow smoothly, while his heart remains pure. Thoughts and actions exist as one. The person who can naturally act in harmony with heaven's wish for the happiness of others and the world—this is the person who may properly be called a Sage.

In instances where we believe we have done something to benefit others, I think it is important that we be careful not to be prideful or look down on those who do not act similarly. It is necessary to plunge one's entire self into the heart of the Universal God prior to taking one's first steps into the realm of 'no persons discarded' that Lao Tsu discusses. If we have any thought of performing actions of love or of doing good deeds, then these thoughts must, in the end, be subtracted from the acts or deeds themselves. This is because the small self that consciously thinks '*I* am doing this' has derailed from the spirit of the Universal God. We only need to know the truth, that the flow of the spirit of the Universal God will naturally express itself through all our actions. This is what is called 'acting in No-action;' it is the realm where all distinctions between God and self— thoughts that say 'I did that'—have vanished.

Entering this state is no easy task, however. This is why I say, for practical purposes, it is enough for people to practice returning all good thoughts of self to the heart of the Universal God via words of prayer so that they may then have their thoughts and actions cleansed and renewed. This is also the reason for my saying that these words of prayer should, like those of the world peace prayer, act to unify oneself with the rest of humanity, while reuniting all human hearts within the Spirit of the Universal God.

The prayer 'May Peace Prevail on Earth' is comprised of truly magnificent yet simple words that spring from the state of 'acting in No-action.' Practicing the Prayer for World Peace thus perfects the union of one's own spirit with the spirit of the Universal God, and links the Universal Heart with the hearts of all humanity. Those who humbly practice this prayer and plunge their entire selves and all their life-energy into its simple words will easily begin performing what would otherwise be the 'difficult' action of No-action, without taking false pride in their own good deeds.

Lao Tsu calls a person capable of 'not abandoning others' or of 'not discarding things' the 'person of Striking Bright.' This is one who has entered the realm of *Mei* (明 Bright), and who has penetrated deep into the heart of God.

Following this, Lao Tsu then concludes this chapter by saying that 'the good person is the not-good's teacher, and the not-good person is the good's resource,' and that 'he that does not value this teacher or that does not love that resource may have wisdom, yet will wander greatly.'

Few will disagree with the statement 'The good person is the not-good's teacher.' Many, though, may have difficulty complying with the second part: 'and the not-good person is the good's resource.' This passage strikes at the very root of Lao Tsu's teachings, however, and these are indeed words that come from a deep understanding of the principle that nothing that appears in this world functions outside the will of the Universal God.

Lao Tsu is suggesting here that a 'good person' will be able to polish his character enormously thanks to the 'not-good's' presence, because the 'not-good person' provides the other with learning material that assists him in improving himself. All obstacles and circumstances inopportune for oneself will in fact cease to exist if one thinks of everything in this way. All things that appear to be working against oneself are thus the training materials that help to further polish and refine one's personality. In contrast, Lao Tsu says that one who regards things that stand in the way of the self as true hindrances, or obstacles, is bound to 'wander greatly,' regardless of how intelligent one may appear to be.

The first step towards a heart that does not discard things is to be of a frame of mind where everything manifest in one's surroundings appears 'good.' As I frequently point out, the easiest method of entering such a frame of mind is to live the life of the prayer for world peace, which includes the recognition of vanishing forms.

By 'vanishing forms' I mean that all thoughts, events, and so on that are manifest in this world are the vanishing shapes, or images, of karmic causes and effects from past worlds. A teaching that enables us to comply with this vanishing process, so that our true, divine Self may shine forth, will, in time, make it possible for anyone to enter Lao Tsu's realm of 'none abandoned, nothing discarded.'

It is the sincere hope of the Lao Tsu deep within me that, via these *Lectures on Lao Tsu*, many may enter this mysterious realm along the gentle, easy-to-practice path of prayer for world peace that was carved out for that purpose.

# Chapter 12

# RETURN TO THE UNLIMITED

*If one knows the masculine yet protects the feminine*
*one will become the ravine under Heaven.*
*If one becomes the ravine under Heaven*
*and does not depart from true virtue*
*one will return to an infant.*
*If one knows the white yet protects the black*
*one will become the model under Heaven.*
*If one becomes the model under Heaven*
*and does not misconstrue true virtue*
*one will return to the unlimited.*
*If one knows honor yet maintains the role of the disgraced*
*one will become the valley under Heaven.*
*If one becomes the valley under Heaven and if true virtue suffices*
*one will return to the uncut block.*
*If this block is split it becomes a utensil.*
*The Sage who applies this becomes a leader of government.*
*Hence, the greatest means of cutting does not sever.*

*Dôtokukyô, Chapter 28*

*If one knows the masculine yet protects the feminine*
  *one will become the ravine under Heaven.*
*If one becomes the ravine under Heaven*
  *and does not depart from true virtue*
  *one will return to an infant.*
*If one knows the white yet protects the black*
  *one will become the model under Heaven.*
*If one becomes the model under Heaven*
  *and does not misconstrue true virtue*
  *one will return to the unlimited.*

The masculine referred to in the expression 'If one knows the masculine and protects the feminine, one will become the ravine under Heaven,' means to be full of courage and of a bright, positive and masculine nature. To 'know' here does not mean to know this with one's head but rather to firmly grasp this state of being with one's heart.

If one can protect the reverse side of 'the masculine'— 'the feminine' (i.e., a gentle, quiet, humble feminine spirit overflowing with motherly love), Lao Tsu says one will then 'become the ravine under Heaven.' This ravine, placed as it is below something as massive as Heaven itself, means a heart that knows no limits, a great magnanimity capable of holding any person or thing—in a word, someone capable of being made into a person of truly great proportions.

If one becomes this kind of giant person—like 'the ravine under Heaven'—and does not stray from true virtue, one will be returned to an infant. In other words, Lao Tsu says that by acting out of a virtue that is similar to the Divine Spirit of God, one is filled with the pure potential and naturally innocent spirit of a child.

Next comes the passage, 'If one knows the white yet protects the black, one will become the model under Heaven.' White is used here as a symbol of purity, cleanliness, and various forms of light mixed together and completely purified. This is a metaphor for the spirit of sagacity itself. And yet, as one makes this spirit one's own, one must also protect the black. The black represents the undeveloped places that light has not yet reached, such as people lacking wisdom.

Since the time of Lao Tsu many hundreds of years ago in ancient China, this earthly world has remained outside the reach of the Divine Light of the Universal God. Today the world continues to be the residence of undeveloped human beings. In other words, it remains a place where people's original divine nature does not easily show through. It is a world of darkness and of ignorance, a world in which the white light does not shine evenly.

If one starkly exhibits this immaculate spirit of the white, one may be unable to mix with others in this world of darkness and ignorance. Towering high above the others, one may become isolated from them and have no influence over the politics and policies of the world below.

This is why Lao Tsu teaches that, by knowing the white and defending the black, by becoming oneself a person of ignorance in order to conform to the lifestyle of others in this world of ignorance, and by then working for the benefit of humankind, one can be appreciated as a person who truly knows the heart of one's fellow human beings and be valued as a fine person of selfless knowledge and friend of all. As models for all under Heaven, such people will influence others, gradually causing them to be purified as well.

The human spirit is a strange thing indeed. There is a Japanese saying that 'Purified Water Houses No Fish.' Similarly, someone who looks up to another as being really fine and worthy frequently abandons the idea of actually becoming that kind of person. Sensing that he could never become such a fine person himself, he views the other as far removed, out of reach, and totally unapproachable.

Lao Tsu says that if we lead a life of 'knowing the white yet protecting the black' and become 'the model under Heaven,' we will not misinterpret true virtue and will 'return to the unlimited.' These words, 'return to the unlimited,' are awesome words indeed. They hold a profound stillness that penetrates inner space, returning us to the deepest-of-deep, purest-of-pure, far reaches of the ultimate. This is the state that I wrote about in the poem called 'Lao Tsu' which appears in the prologue to this book.

This place of absolute limitlessness is the fountainhead of the divine spirit of the Universal God. Therefore, to 'return to the unlimited' means to be made into the divine spirit of the Universal God. I believe this expression points to the true heart of Lao Tsu's teachings.

Despite the fact that the terms *Mu* (無 Nothingness) and *Kuu* are used extensively in philosophic works, it is extremely difficult to convey by words alone such things as the truly amazing experience of reaching limitlessness, or the tireless progression of one's spirit through past worlds to break through and become Emptiness. Explaining this a bit further, one can say that as one plunges deeply into the interior of the physical waves of this world, one will at some point break into the realm of spiritual light. If one fully immerses oneself in this realm, reaching its innermost depths, the world of Bright will be revealed. This world of Bright has numerous levels, which expand through deeper and deeper worlds. Finally, at the innermost of inner levels, exists the profound world of Emptiness, the realm without polarities, the limitless realm of *Kuu*.

The cosmic science I frequently refer to deals with this principle as it applies to the inner realm of the cosmic nucleus, which is the origin of the life-force waves that flow throughout the universe. This is this realm of 'no-limit.'

Whenever I use the words 'Light' or 'Bright' there is a

tendency for people to envision an electric light, the sun's rays, or other light-forms commonly visible in the material world. When speaking of Light or Bright in a spiritual sense, however, we are speaking of a light invisible to the physical eyes. This light is, rather, perceptible by the more sensitive eye of the soul. There are in fact several different levels and layers to this eye of the soul, the distinctions between which are very substantial. This is why there are very real differences between the psychic visions and inspirations of those who merely stand in the doorway to the world of Bright and those who have actually entered inside and are thus nearer to its center. All that is seen and felt by the people of this world, on the other hand, is the movement of the elementary particles, where everything appears as a manifestation of various wave forms.

The science of the world today has advanced to a very significant level. For example, a living object that was formerly viewed only as a collection of cellular particles was then discovered to be made up of atoms. These atoms were in turn discovered to be made up of a nucleus and ions. This nucleus was then found to be composed of protons and neutrons. Mesons were then discovered, soon followed by the hyperon, K-mesotron, pie-meson, mieu-meson, and so on. These discoveries were then followed by the neutrino and light particles said to be the most elementary of all particles. Put simply, what began with the alpha, beta, and gamma rays subsequently exploded into a whole new world of elementary particles.

What was originally called 'electricity' was thus discovered to really be a flow of electrons, and what was termed 'light' was found to be light particles undulating in wave forms. The science of the world today has advanced to the point where it is in fact ready to begin to discover the resonance of the bright waves perceptible now only by psychic vision and inspiration. As a part of the waves of the natural world, these waves will one day be proven to be linked with the others already discovered.

When this link between visible and invisible light waves is proven, what was heretofore only explained in philosophic terms as 'the world of Bright,' 'Emptiness,' or 'Nothingness' will at last be given a scientific base and explained in scientific terms. What is referred to as 'the world of light' or 'Bright,' contains a large spiritual component. This spiritual component—what is called spiritual light—can itself, however, be scientifically proven. This will eventually be accomplished by means of the Universal Particles whose existence we have learned about from cosmic science, through research conducted under the direction of cosmic beings. Among Universal Particles, those that operate on a spiritual frequency (Spiritual Universal Particles) are clearly differentiated from those that work on a material frequency (Material Universal Particles). This is the primary point of difference between the science of the world today and cosmic science.

Returning to the passage, Lao Tsu is thus saying that the Universal Particles begin to function in a wave-like manner in this most central, most fundamental of worlds. Lao Tsu calls this deepest center of the natural universe the 'unlimited.' Using more spiritual terminology, this center can also be called the 'Divine Spirit of the Universal God.'

*If one knows honor yet maintains the role of the disgraced*
*one will become the valley under Heaven.*
*If one becomes the valley under Heaven and if true virtue suffices*
*one will return to the uncut block.*
*If this block is split it becomes a utensil.*
*The Sage who applies this becomes a leader of government.*
*Hence, the greatest means of cutting does not sever.*

One who retains a humble attitude, even when enjoying both wealth and fame, will become an individual of truly monumental proportions. This is what Lao Tsu calls 'the valley under Heaven.' If this same person then accumulates virtue of the Divine Spirit of God, he or she will return to 'the uncut block,' the original tree itself. The person will return, in other words, to the pure and simple world that is the fountainhead of life itself.

To return to the original form or to a pure and simple state does not, however, mean to be used as the raw materials for, nor added as an appendage to, some other product. It simply means to have the potential for being made into a variety of 'utensils.'[18] Applying this to human beings, Lao Tsu says that a person of overly big proportions cannot ever be put to use working for someone else.

Lao Tsu next goes on to state that it is the Sage, living according to this principle, who will become the ultimate leader of government.

In conclusion, Lao Tsu says that 'the greatest means of cutting does not sever.' To cut without severing means that a person whose actions come straight from the original world of the Universal God always maintains a spirit of wholeness, and eventually tends to develop into the most central figure. The true monarch is the best example of this: he or she never acts in a departmentalized manner, and peace will prevail for as long as he or she reigns.

There are a multitude of talents spread among the people of this world of ours. In many cases, these talents are clearly being put to full use. There are also, however, those who appear to be easygoing individuals lacking any special skills, yet who stand out among others.

This is why there is no reason at all for you to feel dejected or give up on yourself because you think that you are clumsy or that you lack talent. By placing your thoughts within the source of the Universal life force through immersion in prayer for world peace, and by leading a pure and simple life in your present situation, you will be made into a person of indescribable charm by the waves of Light that will begin to flow from the Universal Source into your physical body.

Chew well on, and live according to, the following words:

*Believe in your mission,*
*Expend your Human Energies,*
*Heaven helps those*
*who help themselves.*

*Chapter 13*

# ONE WHO KNOWS ONESELF
# IS ENLIGHTENED

*One who knows people is wise.*

*One who knows oneself is enlightened.*

*One who masters others has strength.*

*One who masters oneself is strong.*

*One who knows what is enough is rich.*

*One who acts with strength has direction.*

*One who does not lose one's place will last long.*

*One who is not destroyed at death is long-lived.*

*Dôtokukyô, Chapter 33*

*One who knows people is wise.*

*One who knows oneself is enlightened.*

It is clear from this opening passage that Lao Tsu uses the terms 'wise' and 'enlightened' to mean two different things—that is, one who knows people is wise and one who knows oneself is enlightened. Just what does Lao Tsu mean by distinguishing wisdom from enlightenment?

While it is true that, in this excerpt, Lao Tsu considers knowing people as well as knowing oneself important and probably never intended to make a major point of distinguishing self from other, or wisdom from enlightenment, I think it is safe to say that a natural verbal distinction arose from Lao Tsu's basic belief that to know oneself is more difficult than to know others. To know oneself, moreover, represents a higher stage of development than knowing others. Why, though, does Lao Tsu place enlightenment (*Mei* 明 in Japanese, literally 'bright' or 'brilliant') above wisdom (*chi* 智)?

Let us begin by describing the term 'wisdom' (*chi*). The Chinese character *chi* (智) is written by placing the character 知 (to know, inform) over the character 日 (*hi*, sun). As I have frequently noted, *hi* has the same meaning as the word 靈 (*hi*, or sometimes *rei*, spirit). *Hi* may thus be said to represent the spirit, the original source of light, the original spirit, or original body.

The character for wisdom (智), *chi* in Japanese, therefore, means knowledge placed atop of the essential, divine spirit. This, in turn, may be interpreted to mean 'to know with the head,' 'to know by the experience stored in one's brain,' 'to know cerebrally.' It does not mean to know by the essential, divine spirit or through spiritual awakening.

There is, of course, nothing wrong in knowing with the head, and this is in fact how people generally understand and learn about things. Moreover, people have a tendency to make fun of those who are not good at comprehending things with their heads. In order to associate with and understand others, it is for this reason important to develop wisdom (*chi* 智) and to also have a sound intellect oneself.

Someone unable to understand the true or real personality, who, after only a few words of praise or favors, suddenly considers another to be a good person, or who, upon being reproached, thinks badly of the person doing the cautioning, must be said to be lacking wisdom. This is why Lao Tsu says 'one who knows people is wise.'

On the other hand, while one is able to know people through wisdom (cerebral knowledge), it is impossible to know one's Self by the head alone. To fully know the Self and to see oneself as a living part of the Universal Life Source (that is, to know the real true Self, as distinguished from the visible self), it is first necessary to quiet one's thoughts, deepen the spirit, and enter into the fountainhead of life itself. Without entering the profound state of *Kuu* or *Mu*, the true Self cannot be known. Lao Tsu calls the entry into this state *Mei* 明 (Bright or enlightenment).

Turning next to make a similar analysis of the character *Mei* (明), we find that it can be split vertically, leaving 日 and 月. The left part, 日 (the sun), stands for the positive, masculine, also known as yang; the right part, 月 (the moon), represents the negative, feminine, also known as yin. These principles should be familiar to most. The harmonious interaction of 日 (+) and 月 (–)—Great Harmony itself—is thus represented by the single character 明 *Mei*.

日 and 月 are used to write 'sun' and 'moon' in both Chinese and Japanese. High above earth and far beyond the reach of physical human beings, the combination of these two in the character 明 (*Mei*) depicts the form of Great Harmony as it manifests itself in the highest-of-high, deepest-of-deep, innermost-of-inner worlds at the center of the natural universe. The state of *Mei* may, therefore, be summarized as the state of having entered into the heart of the Universal God. It is a state where there is not even one speck of ego, a state of perfect spiritual purity.

To know one's true Self is for this reason a difficult and, in many ways, incredible experience. As one begins to learn about one's own Self, the individual's thoughts and actions begin to correct themselves, making one freer, less easily swayed by what other people say, and less easily moved by material things, position or feelings. Through knowing oneself, it becomes possible to act out of the essential spirit—the spirit of God itself.

Returning to the term 'wisdom' (智 *chi*) for a moment, there is actually a word 明智 (*Meichi*) in Japanese that combines both *Mei* and *chi*. While this still means 'wisdom' or 'sagacity' it is, again, a term used to represent wisdom derived from divinity rather than from simple cerebral knowledge. Judging from the above, one may readily appreciate the tremendous amount of respect the simple character 明 (*Mei*) commands in the Japanese language.

*One who masters others has strength.*
*One who masters oneself is strong.*

I do not think I need to go into too detailed an explanation of this excerpt, but let us take a few moments before moving ahead.

Just as Lao Tsu says, it requires strength to master others. He is not, of course, simply referring to the strength of one's muscles here but instead means to also include the power inherent in all of the individual's talents as well. This does not mean that someone lacking strength can change the situation by saying things behind people's backs or by saying things to make oneself appear important. There is, in fact, no clearer sign of an undeveloped character than to drop names or to carry on gossip about people in order to convince oneself of one's own greatness.

Possessing strength is, without question, the number one factor in mastering others. The same holds true for relations between countries. Just as between individuals, it is not very impressive for a nation that does not itself possess any real strength to be critical of other countries and act as if it is, in fact, a major power.

A nation's real strength is not, of course, measured by the size of its military. If a nation's people are capable of unifying themselves in the spirit of cherishing their country, and if individuals can place their own personal benefit behind that of their nation, that country's real strength will become quite significant, even if it does not possess military power per se. That is the kind of country I would like Japan and the rest of the world's nations to become some day.

Similarly, I would like to see this kind of energy focused on prayer for world peace. It is clear by now that military power cannot bring forth true world peace. I think it would be far better to re-channel the tremendous energies people are devoting to building up defenses into the movement of prayer for world peace instead. I am likewise confident that our research into cosmic science will be of great benefit to this undertaking in the future.

Lao Tsu says that it requires strength to master others. In

answer to the question of what it takes to master oneself, however, he only says 'to be strong.' As was earlier pointed out, 'to know oneself is to be enlightened.' There is, moreover, no higher state than the state of *Mei* where all desires and karmic thoughts/actions are overcome.

When the true spirit of *Mei* shows itself, an unyielding willpower is born. Willpower that is born from the state of *Mei* is a naturally-spawned willpower, a deep inner strength able to overcome any karmic temptation. This does not mean simply tensing up one's psyche and suppressing desire, but rather indicates a total and free strength beyond the realm of karmic temptations and intentions. In short, to actually master or, as Lao Tsu's original text states, 'win over oneself' is not easy. The kind of willpower needed to overcome all karmic thought waves may only be found by entering the brilliant state of *Mei*.

*One who knows what is enough is rich.*

This passage describes the limitlessness of human desires—of seeking a prestigious position after money has been attained, of craving a still-higher position as soon as some status has been attained, of wanting to always remain at the highest level, and the constant planning and scheming that prevent the spirit from ever coming to rest.

I think that to 'know what is enough' is extremely

important. Regardless of how despondent one's condition, those who are able to find satisfaction within their poverty and who are able to give their spirit a rest have the same spiritual freedom that is often associated only with wealth.

*One who acts with strength has direction.*

This passage means that, regardless of what difficulties may present themselves, the person who has established a path for oneself and who proceeds down it by work and study will, as a traveler with a firm sense of direction, inevitably reach the desired destination.

If attaining that goal is truly the wish of our inner soul and lies within the mission ordained for us from heaven, we will certainly be able to achieve it. For this reason, it is important for us to believe in our own divine missions and to exert our every effort for their completion in the time, place, and situation in which we live.

Because every person has a mission in life, it serves no purpose for people to throw up their hands whenever they find themselves in an environment that does not appeal to them. This sort of attitude creates a tremendous obstacle to the fulfillment of one's mission. Divine power works through people who make their best efforts, regardless of the circumstances, ensuring the successful completion of their respective missions.

*One who does not lose one's place will last long.*

The phrase 'one's place' as used by Lao Tsu here does not simply refer to location, position, or role, but means instead 'the place of truth.' To put this in a very Lao Tsu-ian way, as long as one does not lose sight of the path, one is standing on the Way. Using more modern phraseology, this means being within the Divine Spirit of God.

No matter how high one's position or how splendid one's home, these will always remain ephemeral things— position or lodging in this world that, as part of this world, cannot last more than a hundred or so years. The phrase 'last long' here then obviously does not refer to the relative time of this world but rather speaks of the eternal nature of the person of the Way. This is closely related to the next, and last, line.

*One who is not destroyed at death is long-lived.*

What does Lao Tsu mean by 'not destroyed at death'?

If we think in purely material terms, life is destroyed when the physical body dies. Thus, if a materialist were to attempt to explain the passage 'not destroyed at death,' he or she would have to say that Lao Tsu is referring to the individual's work or good deeds that remain behind in the world for many years following the person's departure.

My reading of Lao Tsu, however, does not allow for such a shallow interpretation of this final line, 'One that is not gone at death is long-lived.'

To not be destroyed at death is to know the truth that life continues, even after the physical body has passed away. Put another way, those who believe that their lives end when the physical body is destroyed do not surpass death. In other words, those people will continue to wander around as if lost in a dream until they realize that, even without the physical body, life goes on in its unified spiritual form. The reverse of this is that many people are now leading what have to be termed 'dead' lives.

A person's physical existence is but a single manifestation of the resonance of life. Human life is, in truth, a creator of worlds. Lao Tsu is, therefore, here warning us about the shallowness of fixing our attention only upon physical forms, and of thinking that there is no human world apart from the physical one.

To enter the bright realm of *Mei* is no simple task. This is why it is important to always live within the spirit of prayer, for this spirit of prayer is, itself, the gateway to *Mei*. And in thinking about the various kinds of prayer, I feel quite sure that a prayer aimed at the peace of all people—a prayer for world peace—is the highest and broadest spirit of prayer that we can have.

The Way is Vast (*Daidô* 大道)
Calligraphy by Masahisa Goi

# THE WAY IS VAST
# YET CAN MOVE FROM LEFT TO RIGHT

*The Way is vast*
*Yet can move from left to right.*
*Everything lives relying on it*
*Yet it does not deny.*
*It only serves*
*Yet is without name.*
*It clothes the ten thousand things*
*Yet becomes not their master.*
*It should be called Small.*

*Everything returns to this*
*But it becomes not their master.*
*If one were to name it*
*It should be named Great.*

*It is because it does not attempt to be great*
*That it is truly Great.*

*Dôtokukyô, Chapter 34*

*The Way is vast*
*Yet can move from left to right.*

What is called 'The Way' here is not a single massive entity, nor is it something that has frozen in place after once spreading out. It is, instead, capable of moving freely from left to right, while still pouring forth like water from a spring. It can move in the horizontal plane to separate into left and right, and is, likewise, capable of moving freely in the vertical plane as well.

*Everything lives relying on it*
  *Yet it does not deny.*
*It only serves*
  *Yet is without name.*

Everything, or all living things, live and grow off the energy provided by the Way. Yet the Way—or to use a more modern term, the Universal God—does nothing to impair or thwart the growth of the ten thousand things, and only continues to impart its life force while leaving everything up to the natural strength of things. Nor do the ten thousand things refuse this life force, saying instead, 'this alone is adequate.' And while God may do such fabulous things as provide life energy to the ten thousand things and give all living things a taste of the joy of life itself, It does not seek fame or in any way become proud.

*It clothes the ten thousand things*
*Yet becomes not their master.*
*It should be called Small.*

The Way, or the spirit and power of the Universal God, is a wondrous and mysterious thing full of love. At the same time, it is responsible for producing the many and varied forms of human beings, mountains, rivers, grasses, trees, birds, fish, insects, and so on, giving them color and illuminating all with the energy of life. The Way does all this, yet also lets every individual be his or her own master. The Way does not make pronouncements that it is the master of the ten thousand things. The power behind everything, it remains hidden from view and it issues no orders.

Turning next to the question of where it conceals itself, one might say that the Way resides and is active within the ten thousand things as Life itself. This is why Lao Tsu says that the Way should be called 'Small.'

Modern science having progressed the way it has, one should realize the profound implications of Lao Tsu's words, 'It should be called small.' Modern science has isolated numerous elements (carbon, hydrogen, oxygen, nitrogen, etc.) that are themselves made up of various particles (electrons, neutrons, etc.) that, when thrown together in various combinations, produce all animate and inanimate things (the ten thousand things). Our own cosmic science has, likewise, identified the Universal Particle as the smallest and most fundamental of all.

The energy that operates within this smallest of entities is the energy of the Way. This is, at the same time, the energy of God. Without the benefit of modern science, that Lao Tsu should choose to call this (Way) 'Small' is almost as awe-inspiring as it is typical of his timeless sagacity.

*Everything returns to this, but it becomes not their master.*
*If one were to name it, it should be called Great.*

In direct contrast to the previous passage, this section goes on to say that 'it' (the Way) should be named Great.

As stated in the lines which precede, there is nothing that lives and grows that does not depend upon the energy of the Way. As a result, everything returns to, and is one with, the Way. And yet, the Way does not present itself as that which oversees everything.

No matter how one views it, the Way clearly does preside over everything, is the parent which gives birth to and rears all, and is the source of all energy. This notwithstanding, the Way does not name itself ruler.

Putting this in human terms, one has to be impressed

with the unfathomable and expansive heart that, while holding such power and all of life in its own hands, does not then choose to show itself on the surface.

Looking up at the millions of stars scattered about the limitless skies, I feel nothing but awe for scale of that spirit. Pondering the great form of the single principle that towers over each of these stars, one has to agree with Lao Tsu that 'it should be named Great.'

The Way is infinitely minuscule and infinitely massive. Just like the Way, the Sage is one who, without having to show oneself, lives sincerely and freely. This kind of person does not hold thoughts that are separate from God, such as 'I am great,' 'I am enlightened,' 'I work for everyone's benefit,' and so on. Nor do such people strive to notify others of their existence. They are, nevertheless, naturally appreciated.

*It is because it does not attempt to be great*
*That it is truly Great.*

We are brought, then, to these closing lines where Lao Tsu says one may be made Great, that is, made into the Way, into the Universal God itself. This, in turn, means that the Sage is someone capable of performing actions that express the Universal God itself.

As I write these essays on Lao Tsu, I am frequently struck with the wisdom Lao Tsu showed in choosing to describe

'God' by the term 'The Way' or 'Great.' I say wise because whenever one uses the word God to describe the Absolute, one immediately perceives God as something separate from oneself, something that is always monitoring one's actions, or something that works to restrict the freedom of the Self. For the same reason, it is not uncommon for people to feel threatened by the presence of something that might level punishment immediately upon those guilty of even the slightest mistake.

On the contrary, the Absolute (God) does not exist somewhere apart from human beings, nor does it do things such as judge them or punish them for their mistakes. The Absolute (God) exists, instead, always within human beings, vivifying them with life-giving energy while assisting them from the outside as well.

By 'vivifying human beings from within,' I mean that God works to make the brain, internal organs and other facilities of the physical body operate. In this capacity, God functions as the life force that sustains each and every individual from within. By 'assists human beings from the outside,' on the other hand, I am referring to God as the Sun and Earth. And when made into air, water and food, God also works to support a human being's physical body externally.

Viewed this way, the power of God exists both within and around human beings. And yet, while this is what made them grow to what they are today, this power makes no demands of, nor issues any orders to human beings in return.

As the Law of Life, God only moves the planets and governs the fate of humanity in accordance with humanity's own self-determined rules. All of the illnesses, calamities and misfortunes present in this world are nothing more than the results of human beings' own discord with the harmonious movement of the universe. They are not punishments handed out by a judgmental God.

It is for this reason that I think that, rather than instruct people about God being the Absolute and the Great Life Force, it may be easier for everyone to understand the truth if one speaks of the Way, or the natural movement of the universe, showing, as Lao Tsu does, how to live and act in accordance with the Way.

Shakson[19] was another who, like Lao Tsu, avoided the term 'God' when mentioning the Absolute. He even went so far as to use a special word, 'Nyorai,' to describe individuals who were enlightened or became one with the Absolute. This was to prevent mixing the karmic[20] thoughts of human beings with the spirit of the Absolute, or the Great Life Force.

I am frequently asked why God made human beings with so many karmic thoughts. These kinds of inquiries are, themselves, nothing other than doubts raised by mixing one's karmic thoughts with the Absolute One, or the Law of the Great Life Force. The Absolute Universal God is, above all else, the Great Life Force, or Universal Life itself. It is the Way. Without giving orders, punishing humankind, or deeming itself protagonist, it is the principle upon which the entire universe revolves.

This is the Way about which Lao Tsu speaks. Though infinitely small and miniscule, the Way spans the Universe and is of limitless proportions. Big, it governs the existence of everything in the universe through a deep, vast array of worlds. Small, it becomes the minuscule Universal Particles and atoms that work within humans and all living things to bring about the movements of life. It is, in short, what breathes life—vivid and energetic life—into all.

The Way is the Law of the Universe and Law of Life. Therefore, all that human beings need to do is live according to the Universal Law and follow the Law of Life. It is enough to live following the Way, acting in accordance with its Law.

But this Way is not readily understood, and the Law of the Universe and of Life are unknown to most. The result of this ignorance is misfortune for individuals and, eventually, the delivery of humankind and the earthly world to the brink of destruction.

The terms 'Universal Law' or 'Law of Life' may appear unnecessarily cumbersome, however, and it is here that we may appreciate the simplicity of Lao Tsu's 'Way' instead.

Simple yet full of meaning, 'the Way' is intuitively compre-hensible to most.

As mentioned previously, there exist both the Way (Law) of the Universal Particles, electrons and atoms, as well as the Way that refers to the lifestyle of human beings. Although Lao Tsu speaks always of the lifestyle of the Sage, there can be no doubt that one's own character will gradual-ly improve if one lives by imitating the path trod by such holy persons. Unawakened human beings, though, cannot easily follow the Way, or the Law of God, unassisted. This is why I have been explaining that there exist Guardian Spirits and Divinities, who guide human beings in the direction of the Way and lend them strength for their own deliverance.

Lao Tsu frequently uses water to depict the Way. Water, with its ability to flow freely into any position and to be shaped by any set of of circumstances without clinging to any single form, leads a truly ideal existence. The word 'vast'[21] in 'The Way is vast...' is an example of Lao Tsu's refer-ring to water to depict the enlightened form of something that can move in perfect freedom, regardless of other people or other circumstances.

Water is not the only naturally occurring phenomenon that shows the way for human beings to follow. The clouds, wind, birds, grasses and trees—all one has to do is study any animate or inanimate thing in the natural world and one's proper path may be discovered.

Just as the scientist pays close attention to the movements of nature and to the movements of animate and inanimate objects in order to broaden the scope of his or her own field of study, so, too, is there a need for people along the way of religion to lead humble and sincere lives, striving for good while taking care, as does the scientist, to observe their own each and every action, the attitudes of others, and the directions taken by all forms of existence.

There is, in Japanese, the expression 'The Way is everywhere,' but if one were to replace 'Way' with 'God,' one would be left with 'God is everywhere.' God resides in all animate and inanimate objects as the Law, and is made apparent by the sincere efforts of human beings in combination with their practice of gratitude to their Guardian Spirits and Divinities.

I discovered my own Way led by my Guardian Divinity and Spirits who had previously branched out from the essential, Universal God, and today I am proceeding down that Way at full speed. This is the way of forging peace on Earth, the Way of prayer for world peace.

The Way of prayer for world peace is identical to the Way Lao Tsu speaks of. Likewise, it is identical to the Way of the Spirit of the Universal God. The Way of prayer for world peace enables people to comprehend the infinitely minute existence of the Universal Particle, and also to grasp a giant key to the Law of the Universe: the way of yin and yang, that manifests the Great Way as many; and the Great Way, that manifests the union of yin and yang as One. This applies even in the infinitely minuscule world of the Universal Particle.

Lao Tsu continues to grow more grand.

# Chapter 15

# IF YOU TAKE THE GREAT ELEPHANT OUT INTO THE WORLD WITH YOU

*If you take the Great Elephant out into the world with you*

*you will meet no harm and your peace will be great.*

*A traveler will stop for food and merriment,*

*but talk of the Way is lean and without flavor.*

*Look at this and you cannot see enough.*

*Listen to this and you cannot hear enough.*

*Make use of this—*

*It may not be exhausted.*

*Dôtokukyô, Chapter 35*

*If you take the Great Elephant out into the world with you*
*you will meet no harm and your peace will be great.*

The 'Great Elephant' that Lao Tsu refers to here is, of course, a metaphor for the Way, or the Spirit of God. The reason Lao Tsu describes the Way using this 'Great Elephant' metaphor is that the elephant holds a natural authority in the animal world, such that even the tiger and so-called king of beasts, the lion, steer well clear of its path. Lao Tsu is not, of course, speaking about the elephants of far away Africa, but constructs his metaphor around the elephants of nearby India instead. The elephants of India are said to be extremely gentle by nature and, while they virtually never initiate attacks on other animals, they themselves enjoy a strong and somewhat aloof position, free from harassment by others. The 'Great Elephant,' indeed, serves as the ideal metaphor for the Divine Spirit as it exists in the animal kingdom.

To 'take the Great Elephant' (in other words, to make the Divine Spirit of the Universal God your own) and proceed along the Way, means to venture into any environment or place without receiving injury or suffering loss of self, regardless of what one attempts. There could be no greater peace of mind than that which stems from the knowledge that nothing can injure or in any way do one harm. This, in short, is the life of confidence that will make for a truly peaceful world.

*A traveler will stop for food and merriment,*
  *but talk of the Way is lean and without flavor.*

'Music' is one translation of the Chinese word 楽 that appears in the original, and the same character can also mean 'merriment.' Lao Tsu is not speaking only of music here, but means to include all of the arts of entertainment that pass through the eyes and ears to please our senses. In a similar way, 'food' here refers to all edible materials that pass through our mouths to bring us gustatory satisfaction.

While these things can draw the attention of and eventually gain control over people, Lao Tsu never alters his tone to accommodate the listener when discussing the Way. His words are, for this reason, 'lean,' or totally lacking embellishment. Without any of the superficial appeal of song or dance, and devoid of intriguing flavors altogether, it should come as no surprise that Lao Tsu's straightforward pronouncements of what people should or should not do were not well received by most. This is because Lao Tsu never attempted to accommodate the listener or alter his words at all when speaking of the Way. The best medicine is that which is bitter to the taste.

Those religious groups that have recently been recruiting

followers at sporting events, or by sponsoring parties under the pretense that life is meant for amusement, are moving away from, not closer to, the Way of Lao Tsu. There are, to be sure, religious leaders who feel no shame in using sweet words and behaving contrary to the Way in order to increase their followings.

As a result of writing these essays on Lao Tsu, I have come to understand from what depth of knowledge and understanding Lao Tsu describes the Way. I have likewise gained a tremendous appreciation for his masterful use of metaphor to elucidate the highest and most meaningful way of life for human beings.

On the other hand, I sense that many readers feel exasperated when they try their own hand at interpreting Lao Tsu's words in their original form, regardless of which chapter they may attempt. This is why I have chosen to write these essays on Lao Tsu, as I hope to take his profoundly difficult, seemingly unrealizable words of truth (or, as Lao Tsu says himself in this chapter, to take the tasteless as well as the superficially uninteresting) and erect a pillar of light which can easily be climbed by the average person.

*Look at this and you cannot see enough.*
*Listen to this and you cannot hear enough.*
*Make use of this—*
*It may not be exhausted.*

I feel exactly the same as Lao Tsu that, even if we see the form or hear the words of the Way (words of truth), these only represent a mere glimpse of the total. Only when we ourselves begin to act does the Way and its various uses become evident.

We enjoy watching and listening to music or dance. So, too, are our palates pleased when we take food. The Way must be acted out by ourselves alone, however, or it will avail us nothing.

In each of these chapters, Lao Tsu has been describing the lifestyle of the person of truth and various profound states of mind. Regardless of how great their truth, though, words not expressed in actions will not suffice. Lao Tsu is first and foremost a person of action, not a preacher. A 'person of action' does not, however, mean someone involved in business dealings or politics. It simply means a person who exists as the Way itself—a divine being—who strikes others with the light of the Universal God.

The Way—Truth—is not to be found amidst extraordinary actions. It lies instead within the most common and mundane of everyday activities.

If we were to take the example of to what we should be thankful for being here today, we might begin by replying that it is the various mechanisms of our bodies continually performing their specified functions that sustain us. According to this line of reasoning, it is our own physical organs that are responsible for keeping us alive here on earth. If this is the case, we should be thankful to our heart, lungs, arms, and legs for working continuously on each of our behalves.

There is nothing strange about this feeling of thanks, and I actually think it is a rather obvious feeling that we should all practice. Most view this to be too obvious a point, however. Not to be led around by my comments to the contrary, very few ever stop to thank the various organs of their own bodies.

I suppose this brings us now to the phrase 'lean and without flavor.' After our bodies, we should next be thankful for the water we drink and the air we breathe. As one cannot live without either water or air, how thankful then should we be for the water and air made freely available to us in abundant supply. These words—'lean and without flavor'— are easily passed over by most as common knowledge, and few indeed are those who embrace such basic things with true feelings of thanks.

By looking closely at each of the things around us in this way, we will discover that we receive nothing for which we should not be grateful. Generally speaking, though, people do not feel grateful to the invisible, untouchable world of nature for continuously providing these gifts to us from the day we are born. By grouping all of these various things together through the realization that it is the divine power of God that breathes life into them all, the spiritual person thus teaches that we should be always sending our thanks to God.

These teachings, devoid of ornamentation and relatively unstimulating, offer no contest to the interesting or entertaining pleasures that more readily draw people's attention. Even among those who turn towards God, faith, or the spiritual, people tend to favor those religious groups that have nice sounding catch phrases or that claim to be able to heal the ill or eliminate poverty with prayer. While this might make pilgrimages possible, it is obvious that people's minds have not changed much from Lao Tsu's time to our own, or differ significantly from one country to the next.

Lao Tsu knew the human mind well, yet continued his elucidation of the way of life that links human beings with the origin of the Great Life Force without ever considering lowering his teachings to match the popular level. Lao Tsu's words have a special, naturally high quality about them. This is why it feels as if the spirit is elevated and made deeper as one reads them—even in the original.

It must be that one is naturally being purified in the process of reading. There can be no doubt that those who received Lao Tsu's teachings directly from him while he was present in this world had their souls heightened by the words—and the flash of light that preceded them—that came from his lips.

Even though I am always with Lao Tsu in a spiritual sense, I feel nothing but tremendous respect for what one must, for the lack of a better term, call the intense strength of a flash of light that, in an instant, can wipe out any karmic thoughts. It is these waves of light that I find so inexpressible in voice or print.

The 'Great Elephant' referred to at the beginning of this chapter ('If you take the Great Elephant out into the world with you') is none other than Lao Tsu himself. Lao Tsu emerged from within the Great Elephant to appear in this world and resolve its problems. Those who understand this are ushered inside him to complete themselves as a part of his mission.

The bright waves of light that are Lao Tsu have been fused with my spiritual body, making me one of those who have had their physical body drawn inside the Great Elephant itself. That is why, ever since being fused with Lao Tsu, my physical self has been unified with my divine Self within the work of the Great Elephant, both striving tirelessly to complete the divine task of raising this world to a world of omnipresent Bright Light.

When a person's divine Self works in perfect unison with his or her physical self, tremendous strength will manifest itself in the form of great works. Lao Tsu, Buddha, Jesus, and the various Guardian Spirits all labor to help create such divine persons.

It is important to discard the idea that Lao Tsu is noth-ing more than an ancient Chinese sage. Lao Tsu is at this very moment sending out intense waves of Bright Light—a part of the light of world deliverance—to help waken each and every one of us. Lao Tsu is very much alive today, and he stands now in the middle of the Way, his white hair of light waving, staring into the hearts of us all. Yes, he stands there staring, wondering if the profound meaning of his lean and flavorless words will sink into the hearts of any, saying to himself, 'how many are really listening?'

Lao Tsu's words are ordinary yet deep, profound yet applicable to our everyday lives.

It is important to remember, however, that words are not in themselves the Way ('Make use of this—It may not be exhausted') and that when 'this' is expressed in actions, it has a powerful, brightening effect on the hearts of others and on the path humanity chooses to follow.

First we must thank our physical bodies. Thank Mother Earth, the Air and the Water—this is the first thing that I hope the readers of these essays on Lao Tsu will do. Let us make the practice of thanks for all things our number one priority and take our first and then second steps toward the ordinary, yet uncommon, life of practicing thanks. By work-ing from within this practice of gratitude, the process of our unification with God will progress.

I think it better, rather than twist around all manner of

theories and philosophies, to have each of these naturally emerge from within the simple practice of thankfulness instead.

Actions are more important than anything else, and a theory without action is an empty, lifeless object. Lao Tsu is a person of action, as I myself am a person who respects such actions. Acts of thanks and of love are basic to the peace of all people on this planet. Prayer for world peace is the one action that combines the actions of gratitude and of love into one function. The words ('May Peace Prevail on Earth') of prayer and gratitude are very, very important in gradually directing us towards world peace. This is why I always include the prayer for world peace in these essays on Lao Tsu, and why Lao Tsu is himself one of the central figures in the prayer for world peace. The truth of this will gradually reveal itself, and we should all join hands, take the Great Elephant, and go out into the world. If we do, our peace will be great and we will meet no harm. 'Your peace will be great'—as will the rest of the world's as well.

*Chapter 16*

# THE HIGHEST VIRTUE
# IS NOT VIRTUOUS
# HOLD THIS AND YOU HAVE VIRTUE

*The Highest Virtue is not virtuous;*

    *hold this and you have Virtue.*

*The lower virtue does not lose Virtue;*

    *hold this and there is no Virtue.*

*The Higher Virtue acts by nothing and holds to no purpose.*

*The lower virtue acts, yet has a purpose.*

*The Higher Benevolence acts and holds no purpose.*

*The Higher Justice acts, yet has a purpose.*

*The Higher Etiquette acts but, when no response,*

    *must lock arms and strike out.*

*Therefore, lose The Way, but gain Virtue.*

    *Lose Virtue, but gain Benevolence.*

    *Lose Justice, but gain Etiquette.*

*The mannered person is of thin loyalty*

    *and is the first sign of disorder.*

*Prior knowledge is the flower along The Way*

    *but is the beginning of folly.*

*The sound person who holds this exists within*
  *that thickness not within the thin.*
*Its place is in the fruit, not within the flower.*
*Therefore, leave that and take this.*

*Dôtokukyô, Chapter 38*

*The Highest Virtue is not virtuous;*
  *hold this and you have Virtue.*
*The lower virtue does not lose Virtue;*
  *hold this and there is no Virtue.*

Though it is common in the orient to use the word 'virtue' (spiritual richness) alone, we can also speak about 'upper' (i.e., 'the highest') virtue and 'lower' virtue as well.

Just what kind of virtue is the 'Highest Virtue?' Unlike the spiritual riches that people consciously try to accumulate through performing good deeds and so on, the highest virtue refers to those things that naturally manifest themselves as virtuous actions without any thought of accumulating a store of good deeds.

'Lower (lesser) virtue,' on the other hand, refers to those actions performed by a person who is always thinking to accumulate spiritual riches and whose heart thus resides apart from the essential spirit of virtuous actions. Even though the actions are virtuous, the term 'lower virtue' implies that this is something different from disinterested Virtue itself.

*The Higher Virtue acts by nothing and holds to no purpose.*
*The lower virtue acts, yet has a purpose.*

The Higher Virtue is performed by a person who acts in all naturalness with perfect spontaneity, not out of an ulterior motive. Consequently, no selfish thoughts of how to use such virtue for one's own benefit, and so on, arise from the person of the Higher Virtue. Lower virtue, on the other hand, is performed with the intention of reaping personal benefit.

*The Higher Benevolence acts and holds no purpose.*
*The Higher Justice acts, yet has a purpose.*
*The Higher Etiquette acts but, when no response,*
    *must lock arms and strike out.*

The higher meaning of Benevolence[22] is that one performs actions without the base intentions of extracting gratitude from others or of using those actions for one's own benefit.

Justice, on the other hand, may be enacted for the purpose of satisfying one's own personal craving for fairness or to receive some reward. The same applies even to the higher forms of Justice.

We come next to Etiquette and see that, even in its higher form, it is possible for people to 'lock arms,' that is, to confront and challenge others in cases where one's own good manners are met by another person's discourtesy.[23]

*Therefore, lose The Way, but gain Virtue.*

*Lose Virtue, but gain Benevolence.*

*Lose Justice, but gain Etiquette.*

*The mannered person is of thin loyalty*

*and is the first sign of disorder.*

*Prior knowledge is the flower along The Way*

*but is the beginning of folly.*

*The sound person who holds this exists within that*

*thickness not within the thin.*

*Its place is in the fruit, not within the flower.*

*Therefore, leave that and take this.*

In this passage, Lao Tsu states that the highest way for a person to live is to live the Way as it is. Those unable to live according to the Way may lead the life of Virtue; those unable to lead the life of Virtue may live the life of Benevolence, and so on. Lao Tsu thus articulates the following order of lifestyles:

*The Life of the Way*

*The Life of Virtue*

*The Life of Benevolence*
*The Life of Justice*
*The Life of Etiquette*

I suppose anyone familiar with the teachings of Confucius will probably have difficulty accepting Lao Tsu's comments regarding Etiquette ('the mannered person is of thin loyalty and is the first sign of disorder.'). However the loyalty Lao Tsu refers to here is far more than the loyalty used when speaking of 'loyalty to one's ruler' or 'loyalty to one's master.' Close examination of Lao Tsu's choice of the character for loyal (忠 *chû*) used in 'of thin loyalty (belief)' is quite revealing. This is a compound written by placing the character for 'middle' or 'center' (中) over the character for heart/spirit (心). Lao Tsu's expression thus contains the profound meaning of the spirit at one with the center.

There are, to be sure, many today who think that this term 'at one with the center' means nothing more than the selfish loyalty called for by Japanese militarist leaders during World War Two. In truth, however, to be 'at one with the center' means to be at one with the center of the universe, or to be One. It implies that to return to the center of the universe, one must first be at one with the center of the essential, divine Self. To 'be at one with the center' is no simple catch phrase.

To return to the essential, divine Self is the same as

returning to the Spirit of the Universal God, or to be at one with the Way. Thus, if a person returns to the essential Being, he or she will be at one with the Spirit of God. Such a person is, in turn, capable of leading Lao Tsu's Life of the Way. The world for loyalty (忠 *chū*) is for this reason an extremely important one.

Similarly, the word for belief (信 *shin*) is, as explained in an earlier chapter, the union of a person (人) with words (言). As words are 'the leaves of God's tree,'[24] this is the same as God and humans being united in the single spirit of Truth. Faith, then, is to be at one with the Spirit of God, the spirit of Truth itself.

Seeing that this original spirit of loyal belief had thinned, there came a time when the leaders and those in power decided that something—even if in form only—had to be done. As a result, they instructed people to show respect for one another by exhibiting certain manners. Manners (etiquette) may thus be said to have been the harbinger of disorder; they were the sign of the coming chaos. This is the meaning behind Lao Tsu's comments about etiquette.

The concept of *Mu-i* is fundamental to Lao Tsu's philosophy. Lao Tsu never praised actions that were based upon human intentions, and did not preach actions based upon a specified form or spirit. Nowhere in Lao Tsu's words does one find him speaking highly of actions that are performed out of something other than *Mu-i*.

Lao Tsu, in this section, thus says that actions of the Way (or actions of the Spirit of God, done by No-action, or *Mu-i*) are the highest actions possible. He then goes on to state that the attachment of any other motive or purpose will only lower the level of actions. The spirit of Lao Tsu is clearly evident in the order he assigns to these other factors (Virtue, Benevolence, Justice, Etiquette). And while I suspect that most modern-day readers will find it difficult to distinguish between Virtue, Benevolence, and Justice, I do hope people will stop to consider Lao Tsu's deep spiritual vision and appreciate his true personal character.

The next passage, 'prior knowledge is the flower along the Way but is the beginning of folly' may be analyzed as follows: Prior knowledge means thoughts that strive to know about something beforehand. This is what is commonly referred to simply as 'knowledge.' Knowledge, however, being different from the Way itself, is like the showy flowers that bloom along the path; if we are not careful, we may become intoxicated with flowery tests of knowledge and in no time be led astray from our original paths. Knowledge, in this way, can develop into 'the beginning of folly.'

The 'sound person'—the person of truth—does not dwell within the frivolous realm of superficialities but is rather always atop the heavenly-lit seat of the Way itself. Not tempted by the attractions of worldly knowledge, that are easily scattered like petals in the wind, the 'sound person' thus remains always in place to bear the fruit of the Divine Spirit instead.

As the self resides within *Mu-i*, Lao Tsu respects actions that are naturally performed out of the mental state of No-action. He does not, on the other hand, hold those who analyze such actions one-by-one with their cerebral knowledge or who engage in various intellectual games in very high esteem.

This is a difficult point about Lao Tsu and yet it will not benefit anyone—either oneself or the rest of the world—to speak haphazardly against knowledge if one is not oneself speaking from the state of 'doing in No-action.' Only those who have perfected No-action and who reside in *Kuu* (空 Emptiness) itself are qualified to adopt such a position on conventional knowledge or wisdom.

When one has entered the state of *Mu-i*, that person's actions are then performed in accordance with a profound natural wisdom. Gradually ceasing to operate with cerebral knowledge alone, and acting in complete freedom, all review by conventional human knowledge then becomes unnecessary.

The problem with cerebral knowledge is that within it lie instinctual feelings of the small self (ego) and of personal loss or gain. These thoughts inevitably block the flow of the Divine Spirit, and turn all one's actions into those of an unawakened person.

Giving this point full consideration, and also realizing that it is all-but-impossible to live in these modern times without such cerebral knowledge, I recommend that people try placing all knowledge within the vibrations of prayer. Lao Tsu, as has frequently been pointed out elsewhere in these *Lectures*, never attempted to lower his teachings in order to make the Way more easily understood by others. My own teachings, on the other hand, guide people one step at a time towards this profound and highest of realms.

When lowered to the realm of Etiquette—to the world of form where matters of the highest of realms are treated separately from the heart—Lao Tsu's Virtue and Benevolence become nothing more than actions of hypocrisy. Once having been lowered into this realm of Etiquette, however, it is most common for people to operate in that world of form only, and to then begin conducting formalized exchanges of greetings and manners. It goes without saying that to have manners based on forms is preferable to the discourtesies performed by a portion of the youth of today; but to build a society upon formalized manners that perform few actions out of the original Divine Spirit is, on the other hand, not very desirous either.

Few, unfortunately, can take the teachings of Lao Tsu and realize them as they are, and there are indeed many who read Lao Tsu's works simply for their refreshing quality.

I do not think it right to relegate Lao Tsu's teachings to little more than psychological refreshment, however, and am, for this reason, endeavoring in these essays to adapt his lessons for ready application in the lifestyles of modern society.

As a first step, I would like to see people perform 'acts of lower virtue' if they cannot perform 'acts of the Higher,' and engage in 'acts of justice' if they cannot perform those of 'lower virtue.' These will be people capable of realizing their own natural etiquette, without having to conduct acts dictated by formalized manners.

While Lao Tsu distinguishes and then, one by one, discusses Virtue, Benevolence, and Justice, I group this together into the single expression, 'the Divine Spirit of God.' This is what I would like to see manifest in all our words and actions. If one fixes solely on the highest of the high, one is likely to experience only misery and discouragement in searching for the Way.

This is why I suggest that people submit all their thoughts and actions to a vanishing process with the words 'Fading away—May Peace Prevail on Earth.' This constant practice enables them to leap straight into the Divine Spirit of God. Prayer is the method for this, and the highest spirit of prayer is prayer for the peace of the world.

Prayer for world peace is the Way—the 'Highest of Virtues.'

# THE ONE OF OLD

*The One of Old—*

 *Heaven holds The One and is, thus, pure.*

 *Earth holds The One and is, thus, tranquil.*

 *God holds The One and, thus, becomes spirit.*

 *The valleys hold The One and are, thus, full.*

 *The Ten Thousand Things hold The One and are, thus, alive.*

 *The Ruler holds The One and is, thus, proper.*

*It is The One that makes these what they are.*

*Heaven without the pure is the tearing open of the truly fearful;*

*Earth without tranquillity is its beginning.*

*God without spiritualization is endless fear;*

*A valley without filling may be exhausted.*

*The Ten Thousand Things without life is unyielding fear;*

*A Ruler without value may be drained.*

*Thus, that with value holds to the base to become the origin;*

 *and that which is high holds to the low to become*

 *the foundation.*

*The Ruler, thus, refers to himself as alone,*

 *deserted and without fruit;*

*But doesn't this holding to the base become the origin?*

*Thus, try to make several vehicles, and there are none.*

*Desire not to become round like the jade nor aloof like the stone.*

*Dôtokukyô, Chapter 39*

*The One of Old—*

>   *Heaven holds The One and is, thus, pure.*

>   *Earth holds The One and is, thus, tranquil.*

>   *God holds The One and, thus, becomes spirit.*

>   *The valleys hold The One and are, thus, full.*

>   *The Ten Thousand Things hold The One and are, thus, alive.*

>   *The Ruler holds The One and is, thus, proper.*

*It is The One that makes these what they are.*

The 'One of Old' referred to here means the person who has attained the Eternal One. This Eternal One is the Great Life Force. It is omnipotent, and holds all potential. It is manifest in an infinity of forms, and is the all-able one that exists prior to the appearance of The Ten Thousand Things. Put simply, this One is the heart of the Universal God Itself.

As the first of all numbers, 'One' is a word used for all. manner of things at present. Yet the tremendous resonance, splendor, mesmerizing quality and unfathomable depths combined with its high-reaching, infinitely penetrating rays that shine to the end of eternity make me certain that 'The One' Lao Tsu refers to in 'The One of Old' is none other than light itself.

When the profound depths and elevated tone of the speaker's spirit reverberate within the heart of the listener— words can be wondrous things indeed. The One of Lao Tsu reverberates within me now as the words of the Universal God.

Lao Tsu says that Heaven will be pure, Earth will be tranquil, and God will become spirit once this deep original One is realized. But, as most probably will not understand the phrase 'God holds The One and, thus, becomes spirit,' let us take a few minutes to discuss this prior to moving ahead with our discussion of this chapter.

The term 'God' (神 *Shin*) does not here represent the Universal God but is, instead, used by Lao Tsu to describe the Soul (魂 *Tamashii*). This is similar to Shakyamuni's use of this same term 神 (*Shin*) to describe the Spirit or Soul (霊魂 *Reikon*). Interpreted in this way, 'God holds The One and, thus, becomes spirit' means that spiritual freedom is first achieved when this original (inner) energy is harnessed by the soul.

'The valleys hold The One and are, thus, full,' 'The Ten Thousand Things hold The One (that is, they are connected to, and live supported by, the Life Force),' and 'The Ruler holds The One (Truth), and is, thus, proper (and becomes, thus, the foundation upon which the nation is built'). In these lines we are shown that the many and varied modes of life and of existence are made correct through their connection with the original One.

Everything, in other words, is derived from the one Universal God.

*Heaven without the pure is the tearing open of the truly fearful;*
*Earth without tranquillity is its beginning.*
*God without spiritualization is endless fear;*
*A valley without filling may be exhausted.*
*The Ten Thousand Things without life is unyielding fear;*
*A Ruler without value may be drained.*

The words 'Heaven without the pure is the tearing open of the truly fearful' are words of truth. Indeed, all calamities in this world are caused by the removal of impurities from Heaven by the power of The One.

Humanity is responsible for presiding over this earthly world, and, in fact, the thoughts emitted by each individual human being are what determine whether this will be a world of brightness or a manifestation of hell. Moreover, Heaven itself may be fouled by the karmic thoughts of human beings as these thoughts grow to envelop this world. For this reason it is necessary to remove these karmic impurities from Heaven when their accumulation becomes too heavy. These impurities are removed by the 'power of The One' (the energy of the Life Force) through an outpouring of energy greater than had previously been at work. Karmic impurities can, in this way, be driven away instantaneously.

The purification of karmic thought waves bring about, in this manner, titanic changes in Heaven and Earth. This is the 'beginning of the truly fearful'—the tearing open of horror itself. And 'Earth without tranquillity is its beginning.'

To forestall and prevent these calamities and disasters, humankind must act by placing all its thoughts within The One. This process of placing all thoughts within The One is what is more commonly termed 'prayer.' The highest method of prayer, in turn, is prayer for world peace. 'May Peace Prevail on Earth'—To live in the spirit of this prayer is the supreme way for human beings to attain The One.

As mentioned earlier, the 'God' (神) found in 'God without spiritualization is endless fear' refers to the Spirit or Soul. Expanding this a bit further, one might also include in this same term, 'God,' as used by Lao Tsu, the various living beings and Guardian Spirits not perceptible to earthly humans via the five senses.

It is common to use the term 'Guardian Spirits,' but this does not mean that these spirits work alone in their job as protectors of the human race. Rather, they work using the power of The One—the power of the Great Life Force—the energy transmitted from God.

It is necessary for physical human beings to constantly lead lives of prayer in order to ensure that these Guardian Spirits continue to work freely, and that the souls of one's ancestors and other closely related persons may do their work smoothly. It is important to steadily live in the spirit of prayer because prayer returns human beings' thoughts to the origin of life, keeps a person always within The One of Lao Tsu, and gradually works to unify the physical being with the spiritual. In this way, even when surrounded by the karmic thoughts of humanity as a whole, the person can manifest his or her original nature as a spirit from God in daily life. And the brightness being emitted will merge into the activities of the Guardian Spirits and Divinities, making their work easier and assisting in the enlightenment of various other souls.

'A valley without filling may be exhausted' means that all natural functions are able to be carried out when we attain The One, but that all works are extinguished where the power of the One does not function.

*Thus, that with value holds to the base to become the origin;*
*and that which is high holds to the low*
*to become the foundation.*
*The Ruler, thus, refers to himself as alone, deserted*
*and without fruit;*
*But doesn't this holding to the base become the origin?*

*Thus, try to make several vehicles, and there are none.*
*Desire not to become round like the jade nor aloof like the stone.*

All existence is, in this way, formed according to the single Great Life Force, the Eternal Life. This holds true for that 'with value' as well as for that called 'the base' ('base' is used here only to denote social position, not in a derogatory way to comment on a person's heart, spirit, or mind). This means that, as manifestations of The One, people of higher social rank should refrain from clinging to discriminatory feelings and hold to the origin in order to join with those of lower social position ('the base'). The high should make its base the low, and should not hold scornful thoughts over distinctions between rich and poor, or the like.

This is why Lao Tsu says that the Ruler should refer to himself as 'alone' (that is, an orphan), 'deserted,' someone lacking virtue, barren, 'without fruit' or happiness. When attaching a title to oneself, one should therefore place oneself in as lowly a position as possible. This act of placing one's thoughts in as lowly a position as possible permits one to make the lives of the base and poor one's guide.

It follows then that, just as the function of a cart or other vehicle is destroyed if one takes it apart to inspect each of its wheels, so too is it wrong to make distinctions between such things as 'glittering jewels' and 'rolling stones.' All existence is a manifestation of The One, the Great Life Force; it is a mistake to attempt to make distinctions between stones and jewels, and so on.

For example, Lao Tsu says that, even if distinctions in wealth or social standing do exist, one should not look upon those manifestations with prejudiced or biased eyes. Everything exists as a single family within life.

The main point Lao Tsu is trying to convey in this chapter is that we need only become one with the Great Life Force (Eternal Life) for all of this phenomenal world to be naturally made harmonious. Wherever there is a lack of this spirit of oneness, some sort of defect will be produced, so that those conditions or those people will eventually face ruin.

Since the time of Lao Tsu, though, the people of this planet have gradually forgotten the blessing and significance of The One. And while there are, of course, individuals who still live according to The One, making the Spirit of the Universal God their own, a single glance around the nations and societies of today is sufficient to confirm humanity's clear lack of gratitude toward The One.

Heaven and Earth and the 'Ten Thousand Things' will, just as Lao Tsu says, be 'torn asunder' (destroyed) the minute the one power that is the origin of all phenomena becomes cut off from the individual's heart and spirit. Our world is in fact now on the verge of such a crisis, and it is not yet at all clear whether or not this earthly world will in fact become severed from the original One.

The crisis spoken of here is the one brought on by the individual consciousness becoming caught up in the physical self, and by each assembly of physical human beings latching onto their own group or country. The result of this is that both individuals and countries seek increased wealth and power (originally bestowed and equally spread around the Universe by the Great Life Force, The Singular-Existent One) for themselves alone. This lifestyle has strayed from the tracks of the Universal Laws as originally set down by the Singular-Existent, and is thus the condition of a disunified heart or spirit. And, as Lao Tsu states, a heart or spirit not at one spells destruction.

Regardless of how one may try to secure powers and accumulate quantities of this or that, these powers and quantities will be destined to vanish away if they do not stem from within the strength of the origin, or if they remain separate from the power and the functioning of The One itself. Proud of its powers and quantities, and constantly attaching itself to the temporary forms of position and power—this is the current state of this earthly world today.

The same can be said about the paths of religion and science. Unless religion and science return to 'The One of Old' they will not be able to live. Without wisdom that is capable of discerning the flow of the eternal river of life, neither religion nor science can offer earthly humanity a true means of deliverance.

Inevitably, it will be necessary to discard all arbitrarily constructed quantities along with the various artificial concepts of God that have been instated by human beings over the past. It is necessary to discard all such things from the past and return to the life of *Mu-i*.

Prayer for world peace is the method for practicing the above. By casting all of one's thoughts into wholehearted prayer for the lifestyle of the Original One, into prayer for the harmony of the people of this world, as in the words 'May Peace Prevail on Earth' and, with a feeling of gratitude, receiving life anew, one can indeed return to 'The One of Old.'

When The One is grasped, the religion and the science practiced by that person will work for the peace of all life on earth.

# Chapter 18

# IT IS AS IF THE GREAT CREATION WERE LACKING

*It is as if the Great Creation were lacking—*

    *yet it is inexhaustible.*

*It is as if the Great Plenitude were empty—*

    *yet it is unlimited.*

*It is as if the Great Right were bent,*

    *the Great Skill crude,*

    *the Great Speech a stutter.*

*Where noise wins there is cold,*

    *where silence wins there is warmth.*

*With pure silence all under Heaven will be right.*

                          *Dôtokukyô, Chapter 45*

*It is as if the Great Creation were lacking—*
*yet it is inexhaustible.*

The 'Great Creation' referred to here means something of large proportions or scale. In the case of a person, this would be a great personality. Applied on a more universal scale, this term refers to the motions of the planets and cosmos itself.

When viewed from the eyes of the average person, it is difficult to comprehend the entirety of something of such scale. As a result, there remains something unsatisfactory about these kinds of motions to the human observer. On a universal level, it appears that there is something lacking in the dynamic and natural phenomena created by an all-knowing, all-powerful God. If God really possesses perfect strength, then the humans born of God should have been made more perfect; the imperfect emotions of anger, jealousy, hatred, fear, and sorrow should, in other words, never arise.

Extending the above logic a bit further, God Itself begins to appear imperfect. But even this conclusion is preferable to those who then go on to say that the statement 'everything is the product of God's power' is false, and thus question the very existence of divinity and the Eternal Law of the Universe.

Viewed from the position of the average person who only thinks about the short-term pluses and minuses of the present situation, someone who expresses the true, Divine Spirit—in other words, a large-scale person, or a person of Great Creation, who is at all times firmly rooted in the eternal nature of life, appears to be unfathomable and not quite 'all there.' Lao Tsu, however, says that the workings of this Great Creation are truly magnificent and, further, that they may not be exhausted.

*It is as if the Great Plenitude were empty—*
*yet it is unlimited.*

The 'Great Plenitude' means something like the ocean or sky that is large and full, something massive and plentiful.

When people become like this—deep in spirit and unfathomable in wisdom—they are often too immense and deep for others. Consequently, they may appear undependable, even empty, to others at first glance. Appearances notwithstanding, their works are, in the end, truly great.

*It is as if the Great Right were bent,*
*the Great Skill crude,*
*the Great Speech a stutter.*

The 'Great Right' means the great divine spirit that runs

through Heaven and Earth, activating and enlivening every-thing. A person of the 'Great Right' only expresses the will and laws of the Universe, never deviating in the least. Yet something as vast as a spirit permeating Heaven and Earth cares little about which way the acorns fall, and lets others do as they like without confrontation. A small-scale person, on the other hand, might make a big issue of something that the person of Great Right considers unimportant, and will go to great lengths trying to force through their own opinion.

Such acts may in fact be interpreted by some to be brave and proper. They can even result in feelings of resentment towards the 'greater' person, who would never act on such petty motives. The smaller person thus comes to look down upon the one possessing the Great Right, saying things such as 'I'd heard he was supposed to be a really great person, but he's not got an ounce of courage,' or 'bowing and giving in to others like that—I really overestimated his character,' and the like.

A person of the Great Right does not favor any particular philosophy, creed, or 'ism' and may for that reason appear only to be replying 'I see, I see' without voicing any opin-ions or objections while listening to others speak. To an opinionated, smaller person, this seems like nothing more than the spineless attitude of a weakling. This is what Lao Tsu means by 'It is as if the Great Right were bent.'

It is as if 'the Great Skills (were) crude' refers to those instances where, on first glance, a work of great craftsmanship and talent appears to be of inferior quality. This sometimes happens with paintings or sculptures, as is the case with the works of famous calligraphers often mistaken for a child's scribbling.

Because a truly masterful work of art expresses a deep, natural spirit, its quality may not be understood through the superficial eyes of the uninitiated, who are drawn more readily to the shallow, dabbed-on colors of a mediocre work. Unless one is an extremely keen practitioner of the particular form in question, or unless one is capable of unconsciously following the movements of Nature, it is indeed difficult to distinguish between true skill and inferior work.

The same can be said about evaluating the true worth of people. A person of perfect truth may appear inept when viewed through the conceited eyes of smaller personalities. Such people of truth can even fall victim to smaller ones' impulse to make fun of them. Ryokan,[25] for example, was a direct and living manifestation of the original spirit of God. Yet, Ryokan led a life that appeared completely absurd to the people around him. Ryokan had the pure spirit of a child and was, for example, fond of referring to himself as *Daigu*, the Great Fool.

To most modern day people, stories of Ryokan waiting for hours to be told he was no longer 'it' when playing games of hide and seek with children, or of allowing bamboo shoots to continue growing through a crack in the floor of his house, or of becoming fond of the lice that gathered on his clothing, and actually counting them with a smile on his face and then carefully returning them back to his clothes, may seem unbelievable. The life-view that lies behind these stories is, however, basically the same as the Great Skill we have been discussing.

The above are all examples of the teaching that 'Great Skill is as if crude.' By this I do not of course mean to say that allowing plants to grow uncontrolled or to let lice go running about freely on one's clothes are in themselves necessarily good. Observing the natural tranquillity that flows behind these stories does, however, provide useful examples of the Great Skill in practice.

The next phrase, it is as if 'the Great Speech (were) a stutter,' is an often-used expression, as it points towards the profound fact that the truth contained in a stutterer's words may move the heart of the listener more than does the polished speech of an orator.

Here the term 'Great Speech' does not mean to wield great oratory through words that flow out with the voice. It refers instead to 'words' that come from a person transmitting the waves of the Great Life Force emanating from the Spiritual Body.

I often point out that true words are not those that arise

from the vibrations of the vocal cords. True words are what exist prior to the voice. True words are, in short, the echoing of the spirit, the resonance of the heart. They are the vibrations of the Life Force, waves of light themselves.

The meaning of the above is that a truly 'great orator' is one who can continually emit these kinds of words, and is not an individual capable of mischievously imposing his or her own thoughts on others. There are, in fact, occasions where this type of truly great 'orator' is an unusually poor speaker. But even if this person is a stutterer, the light waves that emanate from his or her spiritual body shine to fill the surrounding area with light.

This is why we should not judge people by the smoothness or clumsiness of their speech. More importantly, we have to train ourselves to be able to directly sense the unique personal feeling of the other. Once this kind of intuitive sense is developed, one will come to understand the Divine Spirit of Nature and God, the differences between right and wrong actions, and high and low personal characteristics.

It is important to strive to recognize the true Person, and to avoid being led astray by such superficial things as appearances, clothing, words, attitudes, and actions.

*Where noise wins there is cold,*
*where silence wins there is warmth.*

*With pure silence all under Heaven will be right.*

The phrase 'where noise wins there is cold' refers to the state in which a person's true nature is not expressed. Such people are indeed capable of causing a commotion by running and dancing around while preaching this or that 'ism.' They stand in marked contrast to the person of calm exterior yet vibrant spirit, who expresses his or her true nature. In short, this noisy state is one in which life's light ceases to shine, causing us to thus sense a cold, empty place—a place of darkness and shadows only. Many people have themselves had a taste, or have forced others to taste, the cold and empty feeling that remains after the noise and hullabaloo and the self-important talk have ended.

The reverse of this, 'where silence wins there is warmth,' is where one quiets the various thoughts that run around in one's brain and becomes the very center of tranquillity. Putting this into Shinto terms, it means to perform the rite of Mitama-Shizumay, settling the spirit in order to then allow the Life Force to shine as one bright light. The reason that light shines forth when silence triumphs is that the essence of life (the Life Force) is light. Light, in turn, is warmth. The workings of the Life Force are light waves themselves and, in our cosmic science, the very first vibration of life is contained within the workings of cosmic particles.

The Life Force is active. But to allow this Life Force to work as freely as possible—as light itself—one must quiet the thought waves that race round in the brain. This is necessary to prevent the Life Force from becoming enveloped within a smothering layer of karmic thought waves. This is likewise the reason behind various ascetic practices[26] aimed at ushering the individual within the state of *Kuu* or within the 'settled spirit' (鎮魂). It is indeed extremely important for human beings to calm their thoughts.

'With pure silence all under heaven will be right.' The word 'pure' used here includes the idea of pureness as in 'to purify' or 'cleanse.' It also has the meaning of 'original essence.' In Japanese, the character for this 'pure' (清) is written by placing three drops of water next to the character for blue (青). This 'pure' thus literally means 'blue water.' As the original essence of water is blue, water's true essence is expressed when it has been purified to its original color.

In a similar way, Silence, when purified to its original essence, leaves 'the true right under heaven.' Thus, if the nations, peoples, and individuals of this world could only live in a manner allowing them to express their true natures, world peace would naturally follow.

Unfortunately, however, the 'original essence' of most individuals, peoples, and nations, is not yet able to express itself, owing to the smothering layers of karmic thought waves mentioned above. Karmic thoughts conceal this 'original essence,' and prevent most people from expressing this essence as it is. Thoughts allied with the animal instinct of physical self-protection continue to run around inside the head of each individual, greatly affecting the relations between the peoples of this world. As a result, we are still subjected to the spiritual cold that exists wherever 'noise wins.'

World peace cannot be established until this kind of 'pure silence' prevails. What can be done to help foster such pure silence? My reply is that there is no other practical method than to continue one's everyday life within the spirit of prayer. Prayer quiets the karmic thought waves and is in fact the very act of entering deep within the light waves that are the Divine Spirit of God. Prayer is thus a method for making the 'original essence' of one's Self shine brightly, as one of the children of God. It is a method of making silence win out. And, in its highest form, prayer is a means of promoting the peace of our planet—the Prayer for World Peace.

# Notes

1. *Mu-i* (無為), which means 'No-action,' is discussed in Chapter 2.

2. *Dôtokukyô* (道徳経) literally means 'book that teaches the way to spiritual enrichment.' The Chinese transliteration *Tao-te Ching* is frequently used in the West.

3. 'Yin' and 'Yang' are sometimes described as plus and minus energy.

4. 'Sage' is a translation of the Japanese word *Seijin* (聖人), which also means 'saint' or 'holy person.'

5. In the original Japanese text there is no distinction between 'he' and 'she,' 'himself' and 'herself,' and so on.

6. *Kuu* (空) is sometimes translated as 'stillness,' 'emptiness,' or 'nothingness.' Masahisa Goi explains: *Kuu is not a nihilistic or negative condition. It contains nothing, yet everything. It is the infiniteness of life itself, divinity itself, living vibrantly.*

7. *Zazen* (座禅) refers to seated meditation.

8. *Wakôdôjin* (和光同塵) refers to divine light being tempered, or softened, so that it can be more easily received by people in dark (dusty) situations. *Wa* (和) means soft, harmony, or peace. *Kô* (光) means light. *Dô* (同) means same. *Jin* (塵) means dust.

9. The *Kojiki* is Japan's oldest mythological record describing the creation of the Japanese archipelagos and the activities of various divinities.

10. Here, the meaning of 'commoner' is 'unawakened person.' The term *hyakusei* (百姓), which literally means farmer or peasant, is used here to denote the average, unawakened person.

11. *Sûku* (芻狗), the term Lao Tsu uses in the original text, were tied-grass, dog-shaped figures used as offerings when worshipping the gods. These dolls were treated with the utmost respect during religious services, but were thrown by the wayside as soon as the services were over.

12. The Japanese Emperor Meiji lived from 1852 to 1912.

13. 'Shakyamuni ' refers to the saint whose teachings formed the basis of Buddhism. Other spellings , such as 'Sakyamuni' are also used.

14. The character for person (人) is simplified to (亻) when it is combined with other characters.

15. Honen (1130-1212) was the teacher and spiritual advisor of Shinran.

16. Shinran (1173-1262) was a priest who, along with his teacher Honen, established the teachings of the Pure Land Sect (浄土門) of Buddhism.

17. Cosmic science is a scientific study that elucidates the principles and structures of the universe and all forms of life. It is attained by extinguishing the individual self and communing with higher dimensional worlds. More information on cosmic science will be available in the future.

18. Utensils 器 (*ki*): Originally, this word meant bowl—something capable of holding anything that might be poured into it.

19. Shakson is another name for Shakyamuni. See Note 13.

20. Here, 'karmic' refers to disharmonious thought vibrations that stem from misunderstandings about the true nature of a human being.

21. The character for 'vast' (氾) originally meant 'overflowing water' and it gradually came to be used to describe things that are expansive, massive, or vast.

22. The word for benevolence (*Jin* 仁) is written by placing the character for two (二) next to the character for person (人). It denotes the principle of what binds two people (hence, society) together in Confucian thought.

23. The word for etiquette, or good manners, is *rei* (礼) in Japanese, and it is written the same as the word for 'bow' or 'to bow.' To neglect to reply to another person's bow is, thus, a discourtesy (失礼), or the loss (失) of a person's bow (礼).

24. *Kotoba* (言葉) is the term for 'word' in Japanese and it is written with the two characters *koto* (言), meaning speak, and *ba* (葉), meaning leaf or foliage.

25. Ryokan (1758-1831) was a Zoto Zen priest of the 18th century who is still widely loved in Japan for his poems and other writings, which are filled with his love for nature, children, and farmers. Refer to items 178 and 249 in *The Wisdom of Masahisa Goi* (See *Byakko* magazine, Vol. 8, Nos. 7 and 8, September and October 2000).

26. 'Ascetic practices' refer to disciplines such as spending time in the mountains or sitting under waterfalls, and so on, for the purpose of shedding the ego.

# ORGANIZATIONS HONORING MASAHISA GOI

Byakko Shinko Kai
*publishes books by Masahisa Goi*
*and introduces his teachings to interested people*
812-1 Hitoana, Fujinomiya, Shizuoka 418-0102 Japan
Phone [+81] (0) 544-29-5100  Fax [+81] (0) 544-29-5111
E-mail: gbs1357@quartz.ocn.ne.jp
http://www.byakko.or.jp

The World Peace Prayer Society
*dedicated to spreading the non-sectarian message*
*amd prayer May Peace Prevail on Earth*
*a Non-Governmental Organization (NGO) associated with*
*the Dept. of Public Information at the United Nations*
26 Benton Road, Wassaic, NY 12592 USA
Phone [+1] 845-877-6093  Fax [+1] 845-877-6862
E-mail: peacepal@worldpeace.org
http://www.worldpeace.org

The Goi Peace Foundation
*working to build a global peace network uniting our hearts*
*and our wisdom for world peace*
*established in Tokyo with the approval of*
*the Japanese Ministry of Education*
Heiwa Daiichi Bldg. 1-4-5 Hirakawa-cho
Chiyoda-ku, Tokyo 102-0093 Japan
Phone [+81] (0) 33265-2071  Fax [+81] (0) 33239-0919
E-mail: info@goipeace.or.jp
http://www.goipeace.or.jp